£10.

The Autobiography
of Terence O'Neill

The
Autobiography
of
Terence O'Neill

RUPERT HART-DAVIS

Granada Publishing Limited
First published in Great Britain 1972 by Rupert Hart-Davis Ltd
3 Upper James Street London W1R 4BP

ISBN 0 246 10586 0

Printed in Great Britain by
Northumberland Press Limited
Gateshead

To all those who supported me in trying to bring about peaceful progress and change without the intervention of Westminster.

 Contents

List of Illustrations

Preface

I RETIRED from the Premiership in Northern Ireland on 1 May 1969. I carefully considered whether or not I would write my memoirs, and decided, on balance, that it would be better to wait. It was not till the end of January 1971 that I started this book, which was nearly complete in the autumn of that year. A visit to America in October, where I contracted some strange fever, delayed matters still further, and so now well over three years will have elapsed by the time this small scribble sees the light of day.

As I look back, my overwhelming sentiment is one of regret. What could have been solved in peace had to be settled in bloodshed. Continuous one-party rule in any country breeds all sorts of attendant evils. The knowledge that any splits or rows which develop will still leave the party in control of the government, tends to encourage political boat-rocking, in the hope that a new crew can clamber on to the bridge. This is particularly true if a prime minister is trying to carry out long-overdue reforms, in a country where any reform can be described as treachery.

So many things have been written about Northern Ireland in the last few years that it is worth dwelling, for a while, on the advantages of devolution. I was, while in office, a keen supporter of regional parliaments, and in theory I still am. A small area with a regional or provincial government can take administrative decisions, and can take them quickly within the limits of its powers. I remember one occasion when we landed a new industry in Ulster owing to a quick decision taken in the Ministry of Finance. Had we not possessed these devolved powers that factory would have been established in Newcastle upon Tyne. The North East Development Council, who could not move without consulting Whitehall, were not in a position to compete. I have a great admiration for Scotland and its administration in St Andrews House, but I believe they could have achieved more if they

xi

had had a government of their own. The failure of Stormont may well rule out the emergence of any further provincial governments within the United Kingdom but this may well be the wrong conclusion to draw from a particular area with peculiar problems of its own.

Incoming industrialists are delighted to be able to deal with a small local and intimate government. I have never heard anything but the highest praise for our excellent Civil Service. I have seen American consul generals and American factory managers almost in tears when they have been ordered back to America. All Irish people find that they have much in common with Americans, none more so than the Presbyterians from Northern Ireland. They went to America in their thousands between 1700 and 1800, because the British establishment discriminated against them. By the time of the Declaration of Independence they formed a very large proportion of the total American population, and many of their habits of hard work and thrift have descended to the present-day Americans. In fact a southern Englishman has far less in common with an Ulster Presbyterian than an American has. This partly explains our incredible success in attracting American industry to Northern Ireland. When the British Industrial Development Office was established in New York half its staff came from Northern Ireland. Many of these Civil Servants were offered tempting jobs in America while they were there, because they fitted in so well to the American pattern of life.

Several people have told me that they were going to write books on Northern Ireland, but when they have got down to it they have abandoned the project as they have found that both the players, and the rules of the game, change with such rapidity, that even one chapter becomes out of date as soon as it has been written. I must emphasise that this book was finished—apart from some tidying up operations— by the time that Direct Rule was introduced in March 1972. And so it was while Stormont was still nominally in existence that these remarks were written in longhand into school exercise books bought in the village shop in Ahoghill, Co. Antrim. As soon as one book was complete I took it to London to be typed, but I soon found that this system had grave disadvantages, for though I knew exactly what point in the narrative had been reached, I was unable sometimes to remember whether I had already made some observation which I thought was relevant to the whole problem or whether it was still waiting to be included!

The only alternative would have been to have taken a trunk full of material over to England and written the book there, but in a country where cars and luggage are searched this would not have been easy. If, then, the narrative does not flow easily I trust the reader will appreciate the difficult conditions under which I had to work.

The morning after polling day in June 1970 it was obvious that the Conservatives had won the election, but no one knew what their majority would be. At the end of the David Frost breakfast show, I was asked what I was hoping for as a result of the election and I replied 'that Mr Heath should have a large enough majority with which to govern'. When I made these remarks I had something far deeper in mind than the national situation. I was worried that a small majority would hamper Mr Heath's power of decision, and so it nearly proved to be. With a majority even of fifty the Common Market worries would have been less, and Northern Ireland could have been dealt with as London thought best. Later that day on the ITN TV panel, Alistair Burnet asked me to comment on the loss of two seats by the Ulster Unionist Party. They had both been represented by 'liberals' and I expressed extreme sorrow. I went further and said that it bode ill for the future; and then I mused aloud as to whether the Lloyd George compromise solution for Ireland in the Government of Ireland Act 1920 had worked in practice, when we remembered that 75 per cent of it had never come into operation. Suddenly we were switched over to Belfast and there was a jaunty Mr Faulkner assuring us that all would be well and the loss of these two seats was of little importance. He added for good measure that he didn't agree with my point of view at all. Time has, as so often, proved him wrong, and recent events, including the suspension of Stormont speak for themselves.

During 1971 I had lunch with a Stormont MP who was a member of the SDLP (Social Democrat and Labour Party). Suddenly he said: 'Of course the Protestants were mad not to support you, if they had done so Partition would have become permanent.' I had never thought of it like this before, but several times since then I have wondered if there was not some truth in what he said. This narrative will show that personal ambition coupled with bigotry ensured that a huge question mark would loom over Northern Ireland's future, and while I must re-emphasise that my story about Northern Ireland is out of date within a week, I trust that the reader will be able to have a greater understanding of this intractable problem when he has followed this story to its conclusion.

Finally, it may be asked why I didn't write these remarks immediately after resignation. I considered that, on balance, I had better stand back from the political scene for a while in the hope that I could thereby write from a more detached angle. I hope I have, in some measure, achieved just this, despite my great personal sorrow that my attempt to bring about reconciliation was wrecked by wicked men, and that I was thereby unable to inaugurate a peaceful solution to this age old problem.

Glebe House
Ahoghill
Co. Antrim
N. Ireland.

I

 Origins and Background

O N 10 September 1914 my mother gave birth to her fifth child at No 29 Ennismore Gardens, London. Her first two children had been girls and now she had had her third boy. A few weeks later he was christened Terence Marne. It was thought that the first name went well with the surname of O'Neill. The second, which dated him for the rest of his life, was in gratitude for the recent victory at the battle of the Marne.

My father and mother were married in January 1902 and I was presumably to be the last member of the family, for a few days later my father wrote to his eldest daughter describing my appearance and adding that we would soon be like the old woman who lived in a shoe and had so many children she didn't know what to do.

The First World War had been in operation for some five weeks and the great German military advance must have produced much the same anxiety in the minds of my parents' generation as May 1940 did in my own. My father was Member of Parliament for Mid Antrim at Westminster, but had rejoined his regiment, the Second Life Guards, and was soon to go to France. It was in this threatening and unfavourable atmosphere that I first saw the light of day.

According to Burke's *Peerage*, the O'Neill family is the oldest traceable family left in Europe, but unfortunately, and for the record, we are only descended from this ancient lineage through the female line. The last two O'Neill brothers to live at Shanes Castle, the romantic family home on the shores of Lough Neagh, were bachelors —though seldom without female companions. And on the death of the younger one in 1855 the O'Neill estates in County Antrim came to my great grandfather, the Reverend William Chichester. A brilliant musician and an erudite scholar—his musical abilities included composition as well as performance on the organ—he was Vicar Choral at Christ Church Cathedral in Dublin when he inherited Shanes

Castle. His great grandmother had been Mary O'Neill who married Arthur Chichester, the Curate in Randalstown, which is a charming village on the banks of the River Maine, near Shanes Castle. Mary O'Neill's father, Henry, was the eldest son and should have inherited Shanes Castle, but his father, John O'Neill, disliked and disinherited him, leaving Shanes to his second son, Charles. So in fact when the real O'Neill family died out in 1855 the inheritance went back to the senior line, though, of course, only through female descent. There are, however, very few families in these islands who can produce an unbroken descent through the male line, not least our Royal family.

My great grandfather was the fifth generation of Church of Ireland clergymen. I have already described his musical abilities: I often think how much stronger family traits are than people often realise, for at 13 my son, Patrick, took a full church service on the organ at the village of Broughshane, playing on an organ selected by and played on by my great grandfather. Later on he was much in demand to play the organ for services in his regiment, the Queen's Royal Irish Hussars. I, myself, was Captain of the Choir when at Eton, while my sister, Timmy Buxton, and my brother, Brian, both sang in the Bach Choir in London. And there is a letter written by Henry O'Neill, from whom we are descended, begging his neighbour, Mr Dawson, (an ancestor of Major Chichester-Clark) to buy him a voice flute while he was in Dublin. So the O'Neills must also have had their musical leanings.

My mother was called Annabel after her grandmother, Annabel Crewe, who married Richard Moncton-Milnes. When younger he had wanted to marry Florence Nightingale, but knowing, as we now do, how difficult she became in later life, we can think him fortunate to have persuaded this calm, quiet, charming and talented heiress of the Crewe family to become his wife when he himself was middle aged. Their son Robert Milnes, despite a natural shyness and a hesitation in his speech, held at one time or another many of the great offices of State. He become Lord Houghton on the death of his father, who had been created a peer by Palmerston in 1863.

In August 1892 my maternal grandfather, still only 34, received the following letter from Mr Gladstone. 'My dear Houghton, I have to ask that you will give me leave to submit your name to Her Majesty for the Vice Royalty of Ireland in connection with the new Administration. And I hope alike on public and on private grounds that it may be agreeable to you to accept the proposal.*

* Quoted by James Pope Hennessy, *Lord Crewe*, published 1955.

2

Five years previously his wife had died of scarlet fever leaving him a widower with one son and three daughters. Two years later his son died. He was, I am sure, glad to get away from Yorkshire and start a new life in new surroundings.

I remember an old cousin, Johnny Torrens, telling me one evening as we sat alone in my uncle's house near Broughshane, County Antrim, his memories of my grandfather's arrival in Dublin in October 1892. As a liberal viceroy he was unpopular with the Protestant crowds and in consequence mud was thrown at the carriage, which in fact hit my cousin who was part of the mounted vice-regal escort. If he noticed the mud—and my aunt Celia Milnes-Coates has no recollection of it—then he must have realised what was in store for him. He had not long to wait. On Christmas eve there was an explosion under the walls of Dublin Castle and a constable was blown to pieces. *Plus ça change plus c'est la même chose.*

'What a daring dynamite explosion!' wrote Sir Henry Ponsonby, the Queen's private secretary, from Osborne. In a letter to Ponsonby my grandfather wrote: 'The wretched stuff is so cheap and so easy to handle. In this case perhaps 1lb, certainly not more than 2lbs, were used—value perhaps 5s. Yet the street was swept clear and Jekyll heard the explosion distinctly at the Private Secretary's lodge—a good three miles away.'*

For people who have lived through the troubles in Belfast since August 1969 this is a fascinating commentary to read all these years later. Explosions not only wreck the buildings for which they are intended, but they also wake up and disturb tens of thousands of people for miles around. The long-term psychological effects on the population can prove even more devastating than the physical destruction of factories, shops, offices and pubs. Yet it was all happening in Dublin, less than a hundred miles from Belfast, eighty years ago.

It is not generally realised what an appalling responsibility for the state of affairs in Ireland rested, and still rests, on the shoulders of Queen Victoria. She loved Scotland, she loved Balmoral, she may even have loved John Brown. But she hated the Irish. Only in her extreme old age did she modify her attitude, and this was in some measure due to the great gallantry of the Irish Regiments in the South African War. Having refused earlier to create a regiment of the Irish guards, she suddenly gave her assent at this time. While the Irish coach, which we often read about when the Queen opens

* James Pope Hennessy, *Lord Crewe.*

3

Parliament today, was specially built for Queen Victoria's visit to Dublin shortly before she died.

I have always been told that sometime prior to my grandfather's Vice Royalty in Ireland an idea was floated in London with the object of building an Irish Balmoral, half way between Dublin and Belfast. The idea was that it should be an occasional place of residence for the Prince of Wales (later Edward VII) and his family. Furthermore, it would have been within an hour's train journey of either Dublin or Belfast. The Prince of Wales was sounded out and agreed in principle, but Queen Victoria, when informed, soon issued her Royal veto. I cannot prove this story but it certainly sounds horribly likely. In my day and on my initiative a suggestion for a similar residence in Northern Ireland was under embryonic discussion, but the Civil Rights agitation successfully killed the project.

'Irish topics have to be carefully chosen, and, so to speak, peptonised for H.M.'s consumption,' my grandfather wrote to Lord Rosebery, who had by then become Prime Minister. 'It is surprising, by the way, how out-spoken the most loyal Irish are on the neglect of the country by the Royal family. There is a really deep-seated bitterness about it. When I was last at Windsor I mentioned the flourishing condition, and immense size, of the Wellingtonia which she planted during her last visit, fifty-three years ago; but this has been my only hint of the general sentiment. I forget if I told you of the correspondence which passed in 1893, when the Prince of Wales was anxious for the Duke and Duchess of York to come over [later King George V and Queen Mary] and was confident that he could induce the Queen to agree. However, after various appeals she told Ponsonby in so many words that no member of the Royal family should visit Ireland.'*

When the Irish Republic left the Commonwealth in 1949, Lord Killanin said in the House of Lords that this might not have happened if the Royal family had had a home in Ireland. I agree.

Despite my mother's sojourn in Dublin between the age of 13 and 16, she first met my father when she was grown up, with mutual friends in England. She married a young Army officer who had been in the South African War. True the O'Neills had always been Unionists and his father, Lord O'Neill sat on the Unionist benches in the House of Lords, while his uncle, the Hon Robert Torrens O'Neill, was Unionist MP for Mid Antrim, but she was after all marrying my father and not his relations. However in 1910 my great

* James Pope Hennessy, *Lord Crewe*.

4

uncle Robert was told he was dying of an incurable disease and so he decided to retire from what was now becoming a family seat, held for many years by my grandfather before he succeeded to the peerage. My father was then approached and asked to allow his name to go forward. He was not particularly keen to give up the Army nor was he interested in politics as such, and had it not been for the outbreak of war in 1914 he would have retired from the political field.

My mother, who died shortly after the Second World War, often told me that during those four years when he was at Westminster he found himself being used as a bridge. His father-in-law, who became Lord Crewe after leaving Ireland, was Secretary of State for India in Asquith's cabinet and my father was a loyal supporter of Carson and the Ulster Unionists. My mother remained absolutely loyal to the Ulster cause throughout these four difficult years. After her death I discovered in Messrs Coutts Bank in Park Lane, where she opened an account for me when I was 18, a parcel of papers about the period of the Ulster Volunteers when my father had drilled them in the Ballymena area. I handed them over to my nephew, the present Lord O'Neill, and he in turn handed them over to the Public Record Office in Belfast. She had presumably deposited them there for my eldest brother Shane, who was only eight years old when my father was killed.

I was three months old when my father was killed—the first MP to be killed in the 1914 War—so of course I do not remember him. He must have been a simple, straightforward and sincere man. I have never met anyone who did not speak highly of him. His chief interests were those typical of a country gentleman and as you will have seen he was a reluctant MP. He must have been a very nice man, but his speeches in the House were not exciting. He would, had he lived, have become Lord O'Neill on his father's death and have inherited the family home at Shanes Castle. This beautiful place is situated on the largest lake in the British Isles—an inland sea. Until my grandfather died in his ninetieth year in November 1928 it was kept in immaculate condition. Before the First World War special trains were run from Dublin for people to come and see the bluebells. The old Castle on the Lough shore was burnt down accidentally in 1816. At that time great improvements were being made under plans drawn up by Nash, including a terrace built out into the Lough and a large conservatory which was an exact copy of the one Nash built for himself at East Cowes Castle. It survived the fire and is today, I believe, the largest camelia house in the British Isles. It is thought that the oldest camelia trees were planted at the time of the fire. At the moment a motorway is being run through a corner of the large park and one naturally has fears for the future of this beautiful place only twenty miles from Belfast. But my nephew, Raymond, loves it far more than his father ever did, and I hope that O'Neills will be living there for many years to come.

At this stage it would not be inappropriate to tell the legend connected with the Red Hand of the O'Neills which to this very day forms an important part of the Northern Ireland coat of arms. At the plantation of Ulster James I founded the Order of Baronets so as to provide adventurous younger sons with the possibility, not only of landed wealth if they would settle in this inhospitable part of Ireland, but also with heriditary titles to boot. The most famous emblem, the Red Hand of the O'Neills, was selected as the insignia of this new order—but unfortunately some official in London chose the wrong hand—the left hand. I have in my possession an exact copy of a signet ring which once belonged to Turlough O'Neill who lived in Elizabethan times. It appears to be a left hand but only when it is used for sealing a document does it become a right hand. Could it be in this way that London went wrong—as so often in Irish affairs? For centuries afterwards even the Ulster people themselves were misled. Prominent buildings in Ulster like Queen's University, Belfast, are covered with left hands. The Head Line which sails out of Belfast has left Red Hands on the funnels of its boats.

However, towards the end of the last century an antiquarian noticed that the O'Neill Coat of Arms was emblazoned with a right hand and not a left hand. Gradually the correction was made and by the time the Arms of Northern Ireland were created the right Red Hand was made its centre-piece.

But now for the legend itself. It is said that a Viking ship was approaching the coast of the north of Ireland. The captain of the ship said to his men, 'Whoever touches that land first with his right hand will have it for himself.' Two little boats were then lowered from the ship and two sailors rowed for the shore. One of these sailors was called Nial. He was losing the race but he was very keen to have the land; so with his left hand he cut off his right hand—which got rather red in the process—and threw it on to the shore.

Neil or Nil is still a well-known Scandinavian name today and as the Danes founded Dublin, and were wonderful seamen, it could well be that there is some grain of truth in this ancient folk tale. The 'O' which came later is the equivalent of 'Mc' in Scotland and means 'Son of' in modern English. When I was Prime Minister I always wore a tie with a Red Hand on it and when at a function in America I always told the story, usually adding that this was the first real estate deal in history! It went down very well. The Shamrock, whose authenticity is doubtful, is famous all over the world, but the Red Hand which is certainly quite authentic as far as the O'Neill family is concerned, is little known outside Ulster. In all the various trade weeks which we held in many of the major cities in Britain, the whole town was plastered with Red Hands for the duration of the week. I am glad in retrospect that the Red Hand had its little fling in assisting the sale of Ulster bacon, butter, shoes, clothes, textiles and the tourist trade. It is sad to think that it may have made its final appearance in Birmingham in April 1969, a few days before I resigned.

Growing Up

Ennismore Gardens, where we lived till I was seven years old, is one of the few places in London still unchanged from those days. In front of No 29 there is a quiet square and behind an even quieter graveyard set out as a park. It is situated south of Hyde Park on the way downhill to the Brompton Road. But it is to all intents and purposes a cul-de-sac. Hence the peace and quiet. There is a footpath leading down to the shops in the Brompton Road, past Holy Trinity church which we attended on Sundays.

Today it is thought that people with money are those with fast cars, luxury flats and villas in Spain. The cocktail bar and the swimming pool are the signs and symbols of wealth. In those days it was quite different. For one rich family in Mayfair living perhaps in an old family house and with two or three country houses acquired down the ages by various judicial *'mariages de convenance'*, there were forty other families, many younger sons—who could not afford a place in the country or a carriage in London, but who lived in what would now seem large houses. The one thing they could afford, however impecunious, was a staff with which to run their house.

My father and mother started their married life north of the park in Montague Square. In about 1910 they moved to this larger house in Ennismore Gardens. They already had three children and needed more room. No 29 had been bought by friends of theirs for £1,000 a year or two earlier, and they paid £1,500 for it in 1910! Including nanny and a Swiss governess there must have been a staff of at least ten people to run the house. What was normal in those days seems fantastic today.

Families like ours had small incomes compared to their rich relations. My mother had an allowance from her father, Lord Crewe, which covered the cost of her clothes, travel, etc. But her father lived the life of a *grand seigneur*, both at Crewe House in Curzon Street and at Crewe Hall in Cheshire. My father as an eldest son had an adequate allowance from his father and in addition we all went to Shanes Castle for long school holidays. So although there were no luxuries, and no carriage in London, we were nevertheless better off than the children of younger sons, who would have subsidised their small allowances either in the Army or at the Bar or even perhaps in the Church.

One of my earliest memories of London was of the maroons going off to warn us of an air raid during the First World War. As soon as this took place we all assembled in the drawing room on the first floor. My mother had a theory—widely held at the time—that a bomb would damage the upper floors of these tall London houses. Or alternatively would bury us if we went down into the cellar, but that half way up we would somehow escape! I also remember another occasion when my nanny held me out of the night nursery window to see a zeppelin caught in the beams of searchlights. Obviously the maroons had not gone, or else my mother was away, otherwise we would have been assembled in the drawing room and I would have seen nothing.

Nanny Barber came from near Cambridge. I was very fond of her and she was very good to me. We were strictly brought up and sweets were seldom if ever allowed. When she took me out in my pram to Hyde Park she would illicitly buy me, for one halfpenny, a bag of boiled sweets which we both consumed during the afternoon. Later on at the age of about five I was given an allowance of $1d$ a week. By saving every penny I received I was able to buy small presents for family birthdays and Christmas—I don't think I even spent one of these pennies on myself.

One birthday I remember was when my mother took me into her room and there, behind a cupboard, was a red scooter. This was to be my pride and joy not only for scooting about in the park, but also for being a general nuisance on the way down to our house. With my scooter it was possible to come down the hill from Kensington Street and ring the front door bells at such grand places as Moncorvo House, and be a hundred yards further on by the time a distracted butler or parlour maid emerged to find no one there. In time I was discovered and though I am sure my nanny was on my side, I was told that if this habit continued I would lose my scooter.

Soon after my fifth birthday my mother decided that she would like to 'get away from it all' and so in the autumn of 1919 we set out for Florence. My eldest brother, Shane, was at school so he was left

9

behind. But the rest of the family, plus 'Delly', our Swiss governess, set out for a *pensione* outside Florence. My eldest sister, Timmy (Buxton) and the next eldest, Midi (Gasgoigne) both went to school and became most proficient in Italian. Brian, the one immediately older than myself, was forbidden to learn Italian as he was soon to go to school, and so he was supposed to do French with 'Delly' in preparation for this event. Meanwhile, an Italian nurse, Bianca, was engaged to look after me. Inevitably I spoke Italian most of the time. But before leaving London I was told to my sorrow that nanny would not be coming with us, and I don't think I fully understood that she would not be there when we came back. However, I was rather upset both because we were leaving our home and because Nanny was not coming with us.

I have no particularly happy memories of Florence. I quite liked Bianca, I enjoyed talking Italian and singing Italian songs, but to be the youngest member of a family can often be less than satisfying because one always appears to be the least privileged.

After six months, in the spring of 1920, we returned to London, bringing Bianca with us. She stayed on for several months and by the end of the year, at the age of six, I spoke Italian as well as English, but of course it was only a child's Italian, and all I have left today is a Florentine accent with which to formulate a few small phrases.

On my return to London my brother Brian went to school and I went into the schoolroom with 'Delly'. I was not an apt pupil and 'Delly' had a short temper. I can remember on frequent occasions a pencil box being brought down smartly on my head. My visits and return visits seem largely to have consisted of tea with cousins. My first cousin, Jock Colville, later private secretary to Sir Winston Churchill, was nearest in age and the bus journey to Eccleston Square, entailing a change at Hyde Park Corner, was fun. The nursery bathroom there was stuffed with clockwork boats, many of them impressive 'men-of-war' and tea there in the winter was agreeable and included making toast in front of a gas fire. This was something unknown to me in the primitive precincts of Ennismore Gardens where coal fires were the only kind of fire we knew.

Less frequently I went to my O'Neill cousins, but Con* was two years older than me, and even then I felt somewhat overawed by his mighty intelligence.

By now the marvels of Shanes Castle were beginning to impress

* Sir Con O'Neill of the Foreign Office, most recently in charge of our Common Market negotiations.

themselves upon me. It was then and still is, despite all the scars of war-time military occupation, the most beautiful place in the world. After the accidental fire in 1816 there was never a beautiful house with beautiful views, but it had the most wonderful and enormous park of two thousand acres. Until 1932 this included a deer park of 500 acres, but unfortunately today this is a thriving forest of fir trees run by the Northern Ireland Ministry of Agriculture. It is along the northern shores of Lough Neagh that this beautiful park is situated. While the river Maine, having meandered down through County Antrim, flows majestically through the woods of the park under two bridges before it emerges into this vast inland sea.

The main drive from Antrim to Randalstown is five and a half miles long and even when I was a boy some twelve miles of private road was maintained. In my father's day there must have been twice that amount. As one stood on Nash's terrace at the old castle on a summer evening, gazing across the lough to the mountains above Belfast, it was impossible to imagine that, as the crow flies, one was only fifteen miles from the Falls Road and the Shankhill, names unfortunately not unknown outside Belfast today.

The old castle was burnt in 1816. It had reached its zenith in the preceding thirty years. John O'Neill, nephew of the disinherited Henry, was rich, charming and debonair. He was a liberal and his wife, Henrietta, though Anglo-Irish, was brought up near Bath. A grand-daughter of Lord Cork, her father, Lord Dungarvan, died when she was two years old and her mother then married Lord Aylesbury and in this way she grew up at Savernake forest. Mrs Siddons, the actress, was her friend and came and stayed at Shanes Castle when she married. Here is her description of the place:

I made a visit to Shanes Castle, the magnificent residence of Mr and Mrs O'Neill. I have not words to describe the beauty and splendour of this enchanting place, which, I am sorry to say, has been since levelled by fire. Here were often assembled all the talent, and rank, and beauty of Ireland. Among the persons of the Leinster family whom I met here was poor Lord Edward Fitzgerald, the most amiable, honourable, though misguided youth, I ever knew. The luxury of this establishment almost inspired the recollection of an Arabian Night's entertainment. Six or eight carriages, with a numerous throng of lords and ladies on horseback, began the day by making excursions around this terrestial paradise, returning home just in time to dress for dinner. The table was served with a profusion and elegance to which I have never seen anything comparable. The sideboards were decorated with adequate magnificence, on which appeared several immense silver flagons containing claret. A fine band of musicians played during the whole of the repast. They were stationed in the corridors, which led into a fine conservatory which was washed by the waves of a superb lake from which the cool and pleasant wind came to murmur in concert with the harmony from the corridor.

The graces of the presiding genius, the lovely mistress of the mansion, seemed to blend with the whole scene.*

An old print published in 1780 shows a very charming house with Scottish characteristics. Nash was in the process of giving it the 'Windsor Castle' treatment with a huge terrace built out into the lake, when the old house which was to be left intact behind the new building, was burnt.

Once again there is a legend-like story about this comparatively recent family disaster. At the time of the fire a large party was staying at Shanes Castle, and a bedroom usually reserved for the family ghost, 'the Banshee', was pressed into service. It is suggested that when the Banshee came to bed that night she was so angry to find someone in her bed that she burnt the house down. In fact, it is thought that this room, because it was never used, had an old jackdaw's nest in the chimney and that in time the nest caught fire. As it burnt it got smaller and eventually a fiery ball bounced out into the room. Once in the war during an exercise on Salisbury Plain an empty house was commandeered by our brigade headquarters. While the brigadier was giving out his orders there was a roar in the chimney and with a noise like thunder a burning nest crashed out into the room. Here to me was the proof of how the old castle at Shanes had been burnt down.

If the old castle was burnt by accident, the new one was not. After the 1816 fire the O'Neill of the day retreated to his extensive stables. A small Regency house was added to one arm of these buildings and the stables themselves were slowly converted into sitting rooms and bedrooms. Plans were made and remade to build up the old castle on its magnificent lakeside site, but nothing was ever, in fact, done about it.

My great grandfather, the Reverend William Chichester, succeeded in 1855. In the 1860s he pulled down the small Regency house and

* From Campbell's *Life of Mrs Siddons*.

replaced it with a large Victorian addition designed by Lanyon, the Ulster architect. In 1922 the Sinn Feinners set fire to the house. My grandmother, a determined woman, grand-daughter of Admiral Lord Cochrane, managed to save a lot of the contents including the silver which was the one thing saved intact from the old castle in 1816.

It was this old lady who really ran everything at Shanes Castle, because my grandfather was a cripple and an invalid. She was strictly impartial in her employment policies because she pleaded that with her London and Scottish background she knew nothing about Irish affairs. It was a terrible shock to her when the house was burnt. I can remember in her old age she would often say to me: 'After all that kindness they burnt down my home.' Many other large houses in Ireland had military guards at that time, but she refused to have one. At the crucial moment of the fire the head forester, a Catholic, refused to ring the fire bell—kindness did not seem to count in those terrible days.

I was always determined that this early event in my life should in no way influence my outlook on Irish affairs, and it never did, though had I been a 'hardliner' I could certainly have pleaded special circumstances. This goes for the whole O'Neill family. My uncle, Hugh O'Neill, now Lord Rathcavan, who would undoubtedly have been kidnapped and shot had he not been delayed in Belfast that night— he was Speaker of the Northern Ireland House of Commons—was also totally uninfluenced by the burning of his home in any political attitude which he later adopted.

Had I been old enough to realise it in 1921, things were starting to happen at Ennismore Gardens. My eldest sister, Timmy, had 'come out', according to the conventions of the day. A small dance was given for her and dinner parties were given for her before other people's dances. At one of these occasions my mother's first cousin, Lady Helen Graham, asked whether she could bring a charming young friend of hers to dinner, one Lady Elizabeth Bowes-Lyon. Later 'Cousin Nelly' as we called her, became her first Lady-in-Waiting when she became the Duchess of York.

I also became vaguely aware that a certain gentleman was in the habit of visiting the house more and more. He was soon to become my stepfather, but I did not realise that this was to be the break-up of our London home. I continued to regard Shanes Castle as my home, even after my grandfather's death in 1928, when I was fourteen. My mother used to return to Shanes Castle for the summer holidays until my brother married in 1932 when I really became homeless. My school holidays, either from my preparatory school, West Downs, Winchester, or from Eton, were spent either at Shanes Castle or later at my uncle's house near Broughshane or at my eldest sister's house in Epping Forest.

At this point in time I must, however, return to my final year before I went to school. It was an unusual experience for a boy of seven to be swept out from all that he had known in London and County Antrim to Ethiopia, but this is what happened to me. In the spring of 1922 my mother married again at the age of forty, after a widowhood of over seven years. My stepfather was the British Consul in Addis Ababa. After the wedding and a short honeymoon in the South of France, my mother took my second sister Midi and I, accompanied by our Swiss governess, by Messagerie Maritime liner from Marseilles. Through the Suez Canal we went to Djibouti in French Somaliland, and from there a three-day train journey to Addis Ababa, with two night stops on the way.

This year in Abyssinia was undoubtedly the happiest year of my life. The British Consulate in the grounds of the British Embassy was too small for us so we lived next door in the old Imperial Russian Embassy, which was empty at that time. It was a large and spacious bungalow-type building set in its own capacious compound. As one went up the drive to the house one passed the rather sinister tomb of a former Russian diplomat.

My stepfather soon taught me to ride which was almost our sole method of progress in that country. While I had ridden at Shanes Castle, I was not in any way proficient until I had learnt from him. In the morning I was called at 7 a.m. by my houseboy, Gululat. At 7.30 a.m. the groom, Hapt de Wald, would come to the front door with my pony and I would go for half an hour's ride with him, getting back at 8 a.m. for breakfast.

Our governess, still in her early thirties, was naturally much in demand at diplomatic parties, my mother was expecting a baby, and for one reason or another the schoolroom was seldom used for teaching.

In those days the present Emperor, Haile Selassie, was the Regent, Ras Tafari. He lived near the polo ground, half way between the various legations and the town of Addis Ababa. My stepfather had known him well in the province of Harrar where Ras Tafari had been Governor. Soon after our arrival we all set off for a royal tea. We went in the embassy carriage with Sikh outriders. It was all most impressive!

Tea consisted of black tea, bread and honey. It was not very palatable. After the meal was over there was a movement behind some thick velvet curtains and two lions emerged. As a natural reflex I took my feet off the ground and tucked them under my knees. This, however, was too much for the Swiss governess sitting beside me, who slapped them down again, saying that it was a most un-British act on my part. So I had to endure the possibility of losing my feet in silence. At least I knew what it was like having tea with the 'Lion of Judah'! At the meal we all spoke French and before leaving we were presented with golden coins. It was an unforgettable experience for a boy of seven.

The Emperor's eldest son, still then called Mamou, meaning boy, came to my eighth birthday party in September, and he was presented with the full equipment to be a ticket collector on one of the British railway lines! His younger brother, later the Duke of Harrar, was much more like his father, and time may show that it was a tragedy that he did not survive to middle age.

My life was idyllic. I had a giant tortoise which I used to sit on and ride! I had enchanting *duikers* (a small species of antelope) trotting round the house, and none of the discipline which seemed to operate at home in London or Ireland. After a year in which I experienced excitement of all kinds, and during which I became tolerably good in colloquial Amharic, the time arrived for me to come home to school.

One small story bears repetition. It was my practice to go out to children's tea parties at the Italian, German or French legations—none of which were far away. Always I had to carry on my pony a small dark blue tin can containing boiled milk, the top of which was an inverted mug, and of course I was accompanied by the faithful Hapt de Wald. On our way back from a tea party we had just crossed a bridge over a stream about half a mile from our compound when we saw a few tribesmen sitting by the road. It was, I suppose, surprising to see a small boy wearing a pith helmet accompanied by an Abyssinian groom. We trotted by and as the men looked cross and inquisitive the groom stopped to talk to them while I trotted on home. A minute later he spurred his horse and caught me up. 'Bad men', he shouted, and we both raced home at top speed. Inside the compound we shut the heavy gate and were hurrying down the drive when various missiles, including one or two spears, hurtled towards us. Only later did it transpire that they had thought my tin of milk was full of gold!

On our last morning in Ethiopia we set out for the railway station, and although excited about the journey, I was miserable at leaving my dog behind. To make matters worse, as the train pulled out—we were

15

in the last carriage with a verandah at the back—my dog escaped from my stepfather, who was staying behind, and amidst a lot of shouting, etc., it proceeded to follow us down the railway track until it became exhausted. It was a harrowing departure.

3

School, the War and Parliament

I CANNOT pretend that I liked school or that I excelled at any of the activities provided for the pupils. My private school, West Downs, Winchester, was run on scouting lines. The day started with a cold bath, and one of my earliest memories was seeing Peter Scott, then just about to leave, running down a fire escape in the snow with nothing on. He doubtless felt this was called for in view of his father's fame, and we were duly impressed. My cousin, Jock Colville, soon left me far behind in scholastic achievements and when the day came for me to move on to Eton I heaved a sigh of relief.

Here I was most fortunate in having a wonderful house master, A. W. Whitworth. He was most tolerant. My brother, Brian, who later became Adjutant of the First Battalion Irish Guards, and was killed in Norway at the start of the Second World War, bequeathed me a collapsible gramophone. It could be played inside a curious piece of furniture known as an ottoman and stopped by ingenious remote control. So one could be working at one's desk while listening to the latest piece of dance music, but if one was overheard one could pull a string and the music mysteriously stopped. 'No, sir, I didn't hear anything. Do you think it was coming from the house on the other side of the road?' I am sure my house master didn't believe a word of this, but he was sensible enough to co-operate with anyone who showed any ingenuity. When years later I saw all the musical gadgets in my son, Patrick's room at Eton, I realised how times had changed. No sweets were allowed at my prepatory school. No music in one's room at Eton. The Victorian era was still in full swing in the late twenties and early thirties.

After leaving school I went first to France to improve my French and then to Austria to learn German. The family with whom I lived in Salzburg were violently anti-Nazi. The boy in the family, Georg, who was killed in the war, was a youthful supporter of the *Österreicher*

Front and I used to wear its symbols in my Tyrolean hat! It was before the *Anschluss*.

After a year abroad I tried my hand at various jobs ending up in the Stock Exchange. But just before the war broke out my aunt, Sylvia O'Neill—now Rathcavan—who had played a large part in my upbringing as my mother was always abroad, got me a job as civilian ADC to the Governor of South Australia. At that time no army officer was allowed to leave Britain, so that new Governors were unable to find ADCs. For me it was a memorable and happy occasion and I liked both Adelaide and the Australians. The other ADC liked running the house and dealing with all the problems which arose in a pre-war establishment of that kind. I preferred going out and about with the Governor. It was a very interesting experience and I was very sorry when, after a few weeks, the war broke out. With many of the other ADCs in Australia I came back by P & O and joined my brother's regiment, the Irish Guards, when I got home.

On the way back several of us got fed up with the boat and we got off at Suez and spent a week in Egypt, which at that time was still very much part of the British Raj. We then flew back by Empire flying boat, getting home before the ship.

In the last few years I have flown thousands of miles, chiefly to and in America, and I have often thought how civilised were those flying boat days. Not till now with the jumbo-jet thirty years later has it been possible to go up and down stairs in a plane. But far more important, one stopped for the night. On our way back to England we stopped, I think, at Corfu at 6 p.m. and then flew on the next day to Southampton. No violent time changes, no sleepless nights sitting up while a ghastly film is shown to those who insist on watching it. The price of progress is exhaustion!

It is hard for people who do not remember the years before the war to appreciate how strongly people felt about the Government's policy of trying to appease Hitler and Nazi Germany. While in Salzburg in the spring and summer of 1933, German planes would fly over and bomb the town with leaflets. One used to see the Austrian police picking them up in the streets. Still in my teens I became very anti-Nazi. It led, with the passage of time, to awkward family scenes. However, I never had any dispute with my mother on this subject. From the late-twenties to the mid-thirties my stepfather was the British Consul in Sicily and she knew what fascism was at first hand. She was not sorry when my stepfather became Consul General at

Nice. Nevertheless, during the latter part of the thirties appeasement was the official policy of the National Government and those who did not support that policy were unpopular in many quarters.

I wrote several letters to *The Times*. None of them were ever published, but of course we now know that even letters from distinguished people were being suppressed by the editor if they went against the policy of appeasement. Among my friends were the Bonham Carter family. Lady Violet, who later became so well known, partly because of television, was, of course, violently against appeasement and I remember going to an anti-appeasement rally at the Albert Hall with the Bonham Carters.

The other member of my family who like my mother was sympathetic to my view was my brother-in-law, Edwy Buxton. Ten years older than my sister who, in turn, was twelve years older than me, he was old enough to be my father. The Buxtons had a strong liberal streak in their background.

As I have already indicated, I spent a lot of time, after my grandfather's death when I was fourteen, with my sister, Timmy Buxton in Epping Forest. It was while staying there in about 1935 that I was taken to hear the local Member deliver a speech.

My niece, Morna, was to attend her pony club meeting in the forest and at the end of the event the local MP was to address them. I don't think I had ever heard a political speech before, and certainly I had never heard the Member for Epping. When the pony club programme was over Mr Churchill emerged from someone's back garden smoking a cigar. He clambered on to a farm wagon and after a few remarks about the importance of these 'equestrian events'—I had never heard this slurred enunciation before—he plunged into his speech. I seem to recall a sentence which went like this: 'For as I am speaking to you the wheels are turning and the hammers are falling in Nazi Germany.' It was one of his long series of warning speeches which were unfortunately ignored by most of the British population. His audience consisted of about thirty children, their ponies and their parents. I remember thinking at the time what a waste it was that this oratory was being poured out in a forest glade to this small, uninterested audience. And as I was violently anti-appeasement I was sorry that more people were not here to listen to his well-reasoned arguments.

I had been brought up by my mother to read *The Times* from cover to cover and the next day I realised that in politics it doesn't matter where you say something, or whether, at a pinch, you issue a statement, the important thing is to get it printed. In those days the papers had plenty of room and as far as I remember I found the speech on the home news pages almost verbatim. I then learnt a lesson I never forgot, and however much in later life my speeches and statements may have been twisted and slanted, or even transmogrified for the basest political reasons, I cannot plead that they were not printed.

Edwy Buxton had always had a great admiration for Winston Churchill and it was therefore satisfactory for him that during the war he found himself working in his map room. But at this earlier date I think he was influenced to some extent by the views held by his own Member of Parliament.

One further Churchill story from those days is worthy of mention. My brother-in-law's mother, Mrs Gerald Buxton, lived nearby at Birch Hall, Theydon Bois. She was somewhat shy and not over-endowed with social graces. Mr Churchill, their Member, came to dinner. 'How,' she enquired nervously to her MP sitting on her right, 'do you think Britain should be governed?' 'By a triumvirate', came the reply. My sister by this time was all ears. 'Well,' said her mother-in-law, gaining confidence, 'there would be yourself, and who would the other two gentlemen be?' 'That', said Mr Churchill, 'doesn't matter in the slightest!'

Owing to the world situation the Irish question was not in the forefront of people's minds. Insofar as it impinged on my thoughts I was certainly not attracted by the extreme Ulster Unionist point of view. I think in many ways Ulster's first Prime Minister, James Craig, was a great man, but the typical Unionist oratory of those days, 'a Protestant parliament for a Protestant people', was absolutely alien to all my progressive principles.

During the war, however, I began, like so many other people in Britain, to think again about Irish affairs. Here was Britain fighting for her life against the most vile tyranny the world had seen for centuries, and yet the South of Ireland would not even come in with and for America. Lord Longford, in his recent biography of Mr De Valera, has sought to raise the policy of neutrality to one which could only have been pursued by a knight in shining armour. I wonder if this is correct? Supposing that Mr De Valera had refused to help Britain but had welcomed American troops on to Eire's soil, might he not have been true to his principles as well as a better shepherd of his own flock? Instead, when Irish American GIs wished to visit their grannies in Dublin they had to leave their uniforms at the Northern Ireland border. No less than 360,000 American troops were stationed in Northern Ireland during the war. I have often thought that had

President Kennedy been in office at that time, Eire would have found it easier to assist the allies. Indeed, in my view, it was not the policy of the Government which redeemed the honour of Ireland, but the thousands of gallant Irishmen who joined up and fought in British regiments. The majority of the troops in the Irish Guards were from Eire and of course they served in large numbers in every arm of the British forces.

At the end of the war most American and British people were pretty fed up with Eire. Indeed, I remember a Minister in the post-war Labour Government visiting Belfast and saying to me, 'We were very badly advised about Northern Ireland before the war, but today we have learnt our lesson.' The Ireland Act of 1949 which gave Northern Ireland her guarantee when Eire left the Commonwealth, stemmed directly from Eire's policy of wartime neutrality. Since writing these remarks about the Republic's policy of neutrality I have had the honour of meeting Mr De Valera and asking him about this very point. His reply was most surprising to me. 'I lost many good friends during the First World War and had no intention of doing so in the Second.' I made one last attempt to suggest that without coming in with armed support, they could have offered America bases, but I made no impression at all.

In fairness to Mr De Valera I must report that my intrusion of this totally unexpected subject did nothing to spoil the mutual friendship which permeated the visit. Anyone who has met the President will know of his immense dignity. And since my meeting I have frequently asked myself what I would have done in similar circumstances? Had I lived Mr De Valera's life and shared his experiences, hopes and fears, would I have offered bases to the Americans to assist them in their battle to master the Atlantic? I just do not know the answer. It would I think be fairer to leave this to the judgement of history; had I met him before I wrote these remarks on Irish neutrality I might have modified them. Of one thing I am certain, the Republic was most fortunate to have this towering and dominating figure as an anchor in the early years of independence.

After being commissioned at Sandhurst in May 1940, I joined the Second Battalion of the Irish Guards, then stationed at Woking. Our job was to defend a line south-west of London in case of a German invasion. The following year the Guards Armoured Division was formed and we were selected to become part of the Armoured Brigade of the Division. After being retrained and equipped we were always on the point of moving to foreign parts and then finding all was cancelled. However, in the autumn of 1943 it became obvious that we really were getting near D-Day, but at this stage I must digress from matters military.

For many years I had known Jean Whitaker. Her family lived near Lymington in the New Forest and like me she was the youngest of five children. On a visit to her home before Christmas we talked of the possibility of marriage and eventually decided to have the wedding in a few weeks time. On 4 February 1944 we were married in the Guards' chapel at Wellington Barracks and spent our honeymoon at the home of my aunt and uncle at Cleggan Lodge, Broughshane, County Antrim. Jean's introduction to Ireland was sudden, for on arrival in Belfast we travelled in a side-car (a jaunting car) from the docks to the Midland station. We must have been a strange sight, she in her smart London going away clothes and I in uniform, but petrol rationing had reduced the number of taxis available. My uncle and aunt took to Jean at once and were delighted with the new addition to the family. At that time she was nursing as a naval VAD at Portsmouth and was allowed three months' leave to get married.

At Divisional headquarters we had a brilliant Intelligence Officer, Ralph Selby, son of our Ambassador to Austria before the war. He had made a deep study of the German Army and he was now convinced that the guns of the German Panther and Tiger tanks would be able to penetrate the American Sherman tanks with which we had been equipped. These American tanks had great reliability, which could not be said of our beautifully sprung Cruiser tanks, and moreover these American tanks and their predecessors, the Grants, had suited the Eighth Army in North Africa.

However, he communicated to me his anxiety that our new Shermans would be penetrated by the latest German guns, such as those on the Tigers and the self-propelled anti-tank guns. Our problem in assessing the situation was that we did not know where we were going to land on D-Day. If it were on the open plains near Calais then the reasonable speed and mechanical reliability of the Shermans would probably win the day. If, however, it were in close country, then a hidden anti-tank gun of great power would undoubtedly penetrate the comparatively thin-skinned Shermans.

Mr Churchill's visit provided an opportunity for the matter to be raised and I encouraged Ralph Selby to seize his opportunity. On being introduced to the Prime Minister he plunged straight into his theme of 'powers of penetration' and 'thickness of armour'. The Prime Minister, who was obviously surprised by these outpourings, soon lost interest and muttered, 'Speak to me in inches, I do not understand centimetres.' However this may be, Ralph was proved right. Only tank regiments equipped with the much more powerful Churchill tanks could make progress in the close Normandy country known as the Bocage. Indeed, so many Sherman tanks were 'brewed up' that they became known by the Germans as 'Tommy cookers'. Only when we emerged on to the plains of Northern France did we come into our own. And on 3 September 1944 we did ninety miles in one day from Douai to Brussels. But who can say that Ralph was wrong when we remember the enormous numbers of Sherman tanks lost in the first few weeks of the Normandy invasion? The Churchill tanks inspired, and perhaps half designed, by Churchill, saved the day. Whoever advised on Shermans for Normandy was at fault.

After the thrilling capture of 'Joe's Bridge' by the Irish Guards we were on the Dutch frontier by 10 September. My friend, David Peel, who had been best man at my marriage to Jean Whitaker earlier that year in February, won the MC for capturing the Bridge, but was killed the following morning when back at Battalion headquarters, helping his commanding officer to get his sights on to a German tank. Never was a more valuable life lost. He would probably have gone into politics after the war and with his charm and great talents might well have become Prime Minister like his distinguished ancestor, Robert Peel.

Having reached the Dutch frontier south of Valkenswaard, we sat there for one week. We understood that there was no ammunition and no petrol. However, those of us who had eyes to see and ears to hear imagined that it surely would have been possible to supply us with at least sufficient supplies to reach Nunspeet on the Zuider Zee, which became our unattained destination a week later.

Despite my suspicions, I had to wait twenty-one years before I heard the full story. In October 1965 I was the guest speaker at the annual meeting of the English Speaking Union in Atlanta. Our chief public relations officer in London, Tommy Roberts, preceded me and on my arrival at my hotel he informed me that we would be leaving for the opening ceremony in two hours, but that meanwhile General Eisenhower, the President of the ESU would like me to visit him in his suite.

My Private Secretary, Jim Malley, usually went with me on these trips. A much-decorated Pathfinder during the war, he had led the bombers to Berlin thirty-seven times. Looking back on it I think we would both say that this was the most interesting experience in our 'official' lives. After the first hour I asked the General point blank what had happened on the Dutch frontier in September 1944. He paused. 'Yes, I remember it well.' As he still hesitated I suggested that perhaps by this time his relations with 'Monty' were a little frayed —this opened the flood gates.

'I think,' he said, 'that Monty's trouble was that he was a small man physically.' Then, becoming pensive, he said, 'Small men in history have been great.' 'Like Napoleon,' I suggested. 'Exactly,' he said. 'I am afraid I have to tell you, Prime Minister, that Monty was not among them.' While this was all very interesting, I still hadn't heard what happened when we were stranded on the Dutch frontier. 'Well,' he confirmed after I had put the question again, 'Monty told me he would be in Berlin in a week and I had to tell him he was crazy.' Well there it was! What junior officers talking together on the Dutch frontier had imagined might be happening in the highest military places, had actually occurred.

But I had to wait a little longer to hear the full story. I had pieced most of the narrative together in Georgia, but the rest was to come three and a half years later in Belfast. The Irish Guards Association in Northern Ireland has an annual dinner and the colonel of our regiment, Field Marshal Alexander, always came to it. April 1969, a fortnight before I resigned was not the easiest time for me and I had already declined to attend. However, a special appeal came in. The Field Marshal, I was told, had said this would be the last dinner he would attend. His doctor had said he must cease going round the branches. I duly took the hint.

During dinner I had a feeling that once again I might try and fit together any missing pieces from the sad story of September 1944. I repeated to him what Eisenhower had told me in Atlanta. 'Yes,' he replied, 'but Eisenhower was too much of a gentleman to tell you the full story. Monty asked for American troops to be put under his command, and quite obviously, even if Eisenhower had agreed, Washington would never have let Monty win the war with American troops.' However many denials may be issued I am satisfied that this story is fairly near the truth and I am glad I heard it from the Field Marshal's lips one month before he died.

The whole history of post-war Europe might have been different if we could have reached the Baltic in October 1944. The repercussions on Nazi Germany might have been so great that they would have been forced to withdraw the German troops from Italy and Alexander could have gone straight into the 'soft underbelly' so vividly described by Churchill at an earlier stage of the war. Or alternatively had Alexander, with his Irish charm, been the British General dealing with Eisenhower, we might have got what we wanted at the crucial moment when we wanted it. I realise, of course, that the Yalta Conference had already provisionally partitioned Europe, but possession is nine-tenths of the law!

Incidentally, in Atlanta, we found President Eisenhower alert and charming as ever. His heart troubles did not, at that stage, seem to have left any mark on him at all. I doubt if any other man could have played the part of generalissimo in 1944 and 1945 except Alexander, and then, of course, only if we had been the more powerful of the two English speaking allies.

With the assistance of two American Airborne Divisions and our own ill-fated and gallant drops at Arnhem, we tried to repair the week's delay on the Dutch frontier. As history records, we never reached Arnhem, let alone Nunspeet on the Zuider Zee.

I myself was slightly wounded on the north of the Nijmegen Bridge and as we were all cut off for about a week because the slender line to Nijmegen had been recaptured, I spent a week in the hospitable home of the Ten Horn family at Sionsweg 3, Nijmegen. We were all to have a wonderful reunion there years later when I was Prime Minister of Northern Ireland.

Eventually I was evacuated to England and ended up at my wife's home near Lymington in Hampshire, where our son, Patrick, was born in January 1945. I returned to our training battalion at Lingfield in the spring and a month later the war in Europe came to an end. At the end of 1945 I was demobilised.

During the winter of 1944-45 it became obvious that the war would not last much longer and when a sudden vacancy occurred for a Westminster seat in my own county of Antrim I made enquiries about the possibility of being considered as one of the two members for the area. I discovered, however, that all had been arranged. Later in March a vacancy occurred for the Larne constituency of County Antrim for the Northern Ireland Parliament at Stormont and I was advised to come and address the delegates of the Unionist Association who would be selecting the candidate. Looking back on it I am astonished when I remember that I got thirty votes out of two hundred. I had never seen any of the delegates before and only arrived the night before.

After demobilisation at the end of 1945 we moved from my wife's home to Ballymena and made preparations to settle in a delightful

Regency rectory we had acquired at the nearby village of Ahoghill. Here we were only seven miles from my old home at Shanes Castle, and it was pleasant to be so close while the children were growing up. We were in the process of moving in during October 1946 when the sitting member for the constituency of Bannside died and once again I made enquiries. But on this occasion I not only had the advantage of my experiences in Larne, but also as I was physically present, and as my father had represented about half the constituency at Westminster, I was able to do battle on equal terms. There were three candidates and after visiting the delegates I was elected by a substantial majority on the second count. The name of O'Neill had been kept alive by my uncle, Hugh, now Lord Rathcavan, who had represented first my father's old seat of Mid-Antrim, and then the whole county ever since my father's death. For the last few years he was the member for the new constituency of North Antrim, and retired when 'Father' of the House at Westminster.

One small incident during my canvass showed me that political life in Northern Ireland was not going to be exactly what I had anticipated. I was the only ex-Service candidate which at that time in any other part of the UK would have been an advantage, but one farmer when I visited him, told me gravely that he could not vote for me because I was not 'loyal'. When I enquired as to what he meant he said that he would have to vote for a candidate who had been loyal to them during the war by staying at home. At this point in the conversation his daughter-in-law, with a strong Southern Irish accent, denounced her father-in-law. She, it appeared, had served with the ATS although she came from the neutral Republic. 'You are,' she said, 'always talking about your loyalty to the Crown and yet you do not begin to understand the meaning of the expression.' There is, as I was soon to discover, a lot of truth in what she said. The terms loyal and disloyal which may have been useful years ago to include Protestants and Catholics who were loyal to the Crown in the South of Ireland has since partition come only to mean Protestant in the North of Ireland.

After I had been selected as the official Unionist candidate in the village of Cullybackey in November 1946, a by-election was called and I was returned unopposed. Such is the manner of Ulster politics, where you are either in favour of Union with Great Britain or against it, either a Protestant or a Catholic. I was never opposed at an election until I beat Mr Paisley at the Ulster election which I called in February 1969.

4

Stormont

I WOULD like at this point to pay a tribute to the people, and more particularly, the delegates, of the constituency, Bannside, which I represented at Stormont from November 1946 to January 1970. During all this period they stood by me. I never made the kind of violent speech to which they had been accustomed and to which other constituencies were subjected by most MPs, during the whole of my parliamentary career. No other constituency had seen its Member, who happened also to be Prime Minister, make a public and official visit to Dublin and go on television and praise the Pope. Northern Ireland MPs have to be re-selected before every election, and in February 1969 I was re-selected by public acclamation at a meeting in Ahoghill and in February 1970, after taking my seat in the House of Lords, I went to another meeting called to select my successor as Unionist candidate for the constituency, I was given two standing ovations.

Among the leaders of moderation in the constituency were the ladies. Throughout my entire parliamentary representation they supported me, though much of what I did and said must have been strange and foreign to them. My wife was very popular in the constituency with everyone and, what was equally important, she had a wonderful facility for remembering people's names which was of inestimable benefit to me. All of this she did despite the fact that she was not particularly interested in politics or in public life, and would have much preferred to have concentrated on her gardening, a field in which she had become an expert after starting as an amateur. The constant support of the ladies who, as in Britain, work so hard, was one of the corner-stones of the constituency.

I was also blessed with sensible and moderate chairmen and secretaries of the constituency; without them life would have been much more difficult. It is only right that in assessing my time at Stormont I

27

should pay this tribute, for without a faithful constituency I could have achieved little during my period of office. In the spring of 1970 a by-election was fought in Bannside and Paisley beat the official Unionist candidate. Stormont Ministers came down. Speeches were made about good old traditional Unionist ways. Carson and Craigavon's names were on everyone's lips and even my predecessor, Lord Brookeborough, was brought along to speak surrounded by the aura of the Grand Mastership of the Orange Order of County Fermanagh, but to no avail. Paisley won. In June 1970, two months later, Mr Wilson called an election and Paisley stood again, this time for North Antrim, against Henry Clark. Not only was Henry a moderate, but he was an outspoken supporter of mine and he paid the price. In both these elections I dropped a hint that I might be able to help with the moderate vote by doing a certain amount of canvassing, etc but I was gently told that as a 'Protestant traitor' I had better keep out of the way.

Today everyone will tell you that Bannside is an 'extreme' constituency and that that was one of the reasons why I was forced to resign in May 1969. Might I then here say that if everyone had been as loyal to me as my constituency, life would have been easier during the last six months of my Premiership. Moreover, during all material times when I was in political trouble they always sent telegrams of support so that the rest of Northern Ireland could see where they stood. The elderly delegate whom I visited in 1946 may have thought I was 'disloyal' for not staying in Northern Ireland during the war, but my constituency were truly loyal to me, in the English, as opposed to the Ulster, sense of the word.

On my arrival at Parliament Buildings, Stormont, I was impressed by the Building and the setting. I was not quite so impressed by some of the public representatives. The Education Bill, closely following the Butler Education Act of 1944, was the sole topic of conversation. By the time I had found my feet the second reading was over, though many of the back-benchers had given this British inspired legislation a rough ride. The bone of contention was that Roman Catholic schools were to get 65 per cent grants for building new schools. Had some of the more primitive minded back-benchers realised that the Catholics were also going to get 100 per cent of the running costs of those schools their fury would have been far greater.

I decided that I must speak in favour of the Bill, even though the second reading was over. In those days Parliamentary procedure was somewhat less rigorous than at Westminster, and as a new Member I thought that, in any case, I would receive a certain amount of latitude so long as I was brief. I give my maiden speech in full, not because it is noteworthy on a wider stage, but because that Education Bill was to have a dramatic effect on the rising generation. An effect which many people of my generation were quite unable to comprehend when it hit them in the late sixties and early seventies. My remarks, made on 3 December 1946, were aimed not only at the back-benchers who were hostile to the Government's giving grants to Catholic schools, but also at those who imagined that if a Conservative Government were in power, Northern Ireland would have no need to follow the British legislation, and that therefore we should resist the Labour Government on this matter. This is what I said:

I rise with a certain amount of diffidence to speak for the first time in this House, but if you will give me the licence that is usually extended to an honourable Member making his maiden speech I will say a few words.

I rise in support of the Minister of Education in particular, and, with all humility, the Government in general. I should like honourable Members to consider for a moment what the position of the Minister of Education would be were he fortunate enough to be Minister of Education in England. In the first place, he would be a lady Member, and would be entitled to the courtesy and chivalry which I have no doubt are always shown to lady Members in this House. In the second place, he would have but one object to bear in mind, and that would be to produce the very best possible legislation for the future education of the youth of this country.

Unfortunately for the right honourable Gentleman, he is not the Minister of Education at Westminster. Therefore, in the first place, he does not have the protective guard which he might have were he the minister over there. In the second place he has to bear in mind something else in addition to producing the best legislation. He has to consider the various denominational differences which we have in this province, and I think that we should extend our sympathy to him in the dilemma in which he finds himself.

We have just fought two wars to preserve the British way of life, and, in addition to the British way of life, the British parliamentary system which hangs on it, a system which is faithfully copied down to the smallest detail in many foreign lands. There are other systems. There is dictatorship, and we have seen the untimely end to which dictatorships come, particularly the Italian one. There is the policy, dear to one of the large continental countries—*chacun pour soi*—each for himself. That way lies incessant changing of governments and interminable bickering.* I do not think either of those two policies commend themselves to the House. Therefore, if we are to carry out this British way of life, this system which we hold so dear and which we have fought for, we must have some reasonable compromise, some gentlemanly solution for the difficulties which we find ourselves presented with, and I submit that the right honourable Gentleman has tried, to the best of his ability, to come to that reasonable solution.

Would we have the right honourable Gentleman ignore the advice which he received in London, would we have him so irritate His Majesty's Government at present in power that they would be alienated from us? I would remind honourable Members of the House that not only His Majesty's present Government but the people in His Majesty's Opposition have not always quite understood what Ulster meant, and what Ulster stood for. I would remind honourable Members that in 1939 Ulster received a very bad press. Whether you read the *Daily Mirror* or *The Times* you could see unfavourable reference to Ulster, and I consider that it would be very unwise for the right honourable Gentleman to overstate his case in such a way as to cause an unsympathetic response from those with whom he has to consult on the other side with regard to the 1920 Act.

We live in days of bumper power politics and I tremble to think what would happen if we were to alienate the Mother Country, to whom we owe so much and to whom we wish to remain permanently attached. We have a small population in Ulster, and in addition to that we have no provision for making the appalling weapons of modern warfare, nor have we the ability to resist them. I think we would be most unwise to upset His Majesty's Government by overstating our case, and I feel that although it has not come to such a pass, as weeks and months and years went by it might do so if we were to ignore their advice.

To sum up, are we to allow this lengthy legislation, after this long labour, to be wrecked on the rocks of clerical controversy? Let us rather—and I make this appeal in all humility—close our

* After the war French Governments changed with extreme rapidity.

ranks, sink our differences, pull together and determine that it will be possible for a man or a woman born in Ulster, and finding himself or herself in future in some distant part of the British Commonwealth, or even in some foreign land, to say with pride, 'I was educated in Ulster.'

In February 1948 I became Parliamentary Secretary to William Grant, who was then Minister of Health. He had been a shipyard worker, and although a strong Protestant, he was all in favour of the British Welfare State. When he introduced his Health Bill in 1947 I was one of the few Unionist back-benchers who supported it, and so he was, I think, happy when I joined him a few months later. Only some 1,100 houses had been built in 1947, and Billy Grant, whose Ministry was responsible for housing, had made some acrimonious remarks about the fact that more houses would have been built if only the materials had been procured. As the Works branch of the Ministry of Finance were responsible for obtaining supplies, such as cement from England, the Minister of Finance, Maynard Sinclair, was understandably incensed. I went to the Ministry with a special responsibility for housing. It was only when I got there that I discovered I was also to act as special link between the Ministry of Health and the Ministry of Finance!

Northern Ireland had, from towards the end of the war till it was tragically wound up in October 1971 as a result of reforms, a 'housing trust'; not unlike the Scottish Special Housing Association, under the chairmanship of Sir Lucius O'Brien. It did sterling work. It introduced new firms from across the Channel who helped to bust the building ring which inevitably existed in a small place like Northern Ireland: while it had the courage to build houses for Catholics in areas where the local councils were too frightened to build in case they were turned out by their supporters. It raised housing standards and set an example to councils whose record of house building was little short of scandalous.

Unfortunately the Ministry of Finance, at that time, were hostile to the trust and I fought many battles to stop its being wound up. As I hadn't set it up myself and as my background was not particularly socialistic, I was able to parry suggestions that it was pure socialism and that if the Labour Government didn't have a housing trust in England why should we have one here. My only sorrow is that the housing trust did not build on a larger scale. But make no mistake about it, with the facilities that we then had—planning and new town

techniques were virtually non-existent—and with the frightfully reactionary attitudes of that time, we were very fortunate indeed to
have the trust and many people who are living in trust houses today
should realise that but for the progressive outlook of the Ministry of
Health and its early effort to break down sectarianism, to set high
standards of design and planning and to build about one-third of the
annual number of houses in those early days, things would have been
much worse than they were.

By the end of 1948 the house completion rate had risen to nearly
5,000. Anyone who has dealt with housing knows that you can only
get a good completion rate if you have a good rate of 'starts'. So in a
sense we were fortunate. In any case, we were all pleased, none more
so than Billy Grant himself.

In August 1949 Grant, who had frequently been ill, died. I liked
him. He was a typical Belfast Protestant working man, strongly anti-
Catholic, but decent. It will be recalled that when Winston Churchill
visited Belfast to address a Liberal meeting in 1912 his car was nearly
overturned. I remember Billy telling me that he was one of the shipyard workers involved. They had every intention of killing Churchill,
till suddenly they saw his wife beside him and that cooled them down.
Could these Belfast shipyard workers have altered the course of history
in 1940? I think when we remember the alternative candidates for
the Premiership at that time, we must agree that no one else could
have evoked the Dunkirk spirit in quite the same manner, and without
it we might have been defeated.

Grant was succeeded as Minister by Dame Dehra Parker, the grandmother of my successor, James Chichester-Clark. We had a lot in
common, not least an interest in the arts, but I must admit that I
spent four frustrating years as her parliamentary secretary. This was
chiefly because I was really not allowed to do anything in public,
though my advice was constantly sought in private. Sixty-eight when
she was appointed, she was always about to resign—but never did!
However, with increasing bouts of illness I found I was constantly
fulfilling her public engagements at the last minute.

In 1953 I was shifted, against my will, to the Chairmanship of Ways
and Means, where I spent two more years not so much of frustration
as of inaction. It was at this time that I started growing specimen
trees in a field, which when I am feeling grand I describe as my
arboretum, and when humble as my field. It was in 1954 that I had
the good fortune to go on a Commonwealth Tour of Africa. A
Conference was held in Nairobi and we also visited Uganda, Tanga-

nyika, Northern Rhodesia, Southern Rhodesia and all the four Provinces of the Union—I also have a vivid memory of staying at Government House in Salisbury. At the various functions held there I remember senior government servants talking to me about the importance of 'federation' and 'partnership'. Almost forgotten words today. How wrong can people be? Or to put it in another way, how often are politicians or civil servants right?

In 1955 I was approached by the then Minister of Home Affairs, George Hanna, and asked if I would return to the Government as joint Parliamentary Secretary to him and to Dame Dehra? I was reluctant to return to Health, but went to consult the Permanent Secretary, Freer, a man for whom I had a considerable regard. He begged me to return saying that Dame Dehra was determined to introduce a Measure of Rent De-restriction ahead of certain Westminster legislation, that the details of the Bill would be complex and that at her age and in her state of health he doubted whether she could manage it. This plea worked and I decided to go back into the Government.

I soon decided that Freer was right and that to precede Westminster in a Rent De-restriction Bill, when we had already had a small one a year or two previously, would not be wise. I decided to visit my opposite number at Westminster and ask his advice. The parliamentary secretary in question was a certain Mr Enoch Powell. My private secretary spoke to his, and a meeting was arranged. I had on several occasions visited various 'opposite numbers' when I had been in the Ministry of Health before, but always in their offices with civil servants present. But on this occasion I was told that Mr Powell would like to give me dinner at the House of Commons as he was too busy to see me in his office. I was delighted. However, when I had consulted *Who's Who* and noted his qualifications I was anxious as to whether I could hold my own even in ordinary conversation.

I went. He gave me an excellent dinner and refused to talk shop. After dinner over coffee, port and cigars he asked me what was on my mind. I told him and he considered my problem and then gave me excellent advice. 'If,' he said, 'you go ahead of us in this measure and get into trouble which receives publicity in the British press, then this will make our task difficult. If, however, you follow in our wake when we have blazed the trail, then you can justify your actions without risking your chances or possibly spoiling ours.' He was charming and wise, and, I somehow feel, quite a different person to the one he has now become.

I returned in triumph and told the permanent secretary that Whitehall agreed with us, but we both underestimated the determination of our minister. She insisted on going ahead. One day later when we were alone she said to me, 'Terence, you don't understand, this measure will be a monument to me.' 'Yes,' I replied, 'but I'm afraid it could be your tombstone.' The battle raged all through the winter and as Enoch had feared it was reported in the British press. At a crucial moment in these affairs the Attorney General, Edmund Warnock, who at an earlier stage had demanded and been granted a Party meeting in order to discuss the alteration of the licensing hours which George Hanna was intending to introduce, threw down the gauntlet, and the Prime Minister, Lord Brookeborough, beat one of his usual retreats. But in the end, realising that both his Minister of Home Affairs and his Minister of Health would resign if the Bill were entirely dropped—instead of being modified—he had to part company with his Attorney General. The then Minister of Finance, Brian Maginnis, became Attorney General and George Hanna became Minister of Finance, while I became Minister of Home Affairs.

Had Dame Dehra followed my advice, and incidentally Enoch Powell's advice, the Attorney General would never have resigned and in consequence I would not have become Minister of Home Affairs at the age of 42 in the spring of 1956. In the autumn of 1956 George Hanna, who had only been Minister of Finance for six months, was warned by his doctor he should retire from politics. Moreover, he had not, as a lawyer, been happy in Finance. A vacancy occurred in the County Court of Down and he was glad to retire from the political scene. I was asked to take on Finance as well as Home Affairs and so from having been a parliamentary secretary for far too long I suddenly found myself holding both the most senior positions in the Cabinet within six months of joining it.

Holding two ministries is, in my view, wrong, but it is a favourite Northern Ireland habit. Brian Maginnis, by then Attorney General, had been at an earlier stage joint Minister of Finance and Home Affairs for over a year, so I was determined that the same should not happen to me. In any case, I was far happier in Finance than I was in Home Affairs so after about six weeks I made it plain that I would not go on holding the two positions much longer and a successor, Ken Topping, replaced me in Home Affairs. This started a very happy period for me in the Ministry of Finance.

5

Finance

ON my arrival at the Ministry of Finance I found there an excellent Private Secretary, Ken Bloomfield. This Oxford man, born of English parents in Belfast, soon became a close friend. While fully understanding the Ulster outlook, his English origins made it possible for him to see things in a wider context. As history was his subject he could better understand the problems with which we were faced than many civil servants whose whole background lay in Northern Ireland. After three years he went to New York to become the first assistant director of the British Industrial Development Office in America. He was the obvious man for the job, but I was personally sorry to see him go. His successor, Jim Malley, whom I mention later in the narrative, was with me till I resigned the Premiership nine years later. Seldom has a minister been better served than I was by these two men. When I became Prime Minister I brought Bloomfield back from New York, soon to become No 2 in the Cabinet offices.

The Ministry of Finance encompassed a wide variety of activities. It had a Works branch doing the job of the old Ministry of Works in London, this included Government buildings and ancient monuments. The Ministry also controlled the Civil Service and the permanent secretary, known in Northern Ireland as the Secretary, was the head of the Civil Service. It was in every way the controlling Ministry, and Cabinet memoranda had to be submitted to the Ministry before they went to the Cabinet offices for circulation. The Minister of Finance was second in seniority to the Prime Minister and acted for him when he was away. I did six and a half years in this job and during that period I dealt with five Tory Chancellors from Macmillan to Maudling. On Budget morning in London one visits the Treasury and is given the main details of the Budget along with the Secretary of the Ministry from Northern Ireland. So apart from the

Queen and the Cabinet the Minister of Finance is the only person who knows the Budget secrets. At first I was guided by the charming and helpful Edmund Compton, later to become Ombudsman both of Great Britain and Northern Ireland. Afterwards, for many years, the Treasury official who briefed me was William Armstrong, then head of Home Finance in the Treasury, and now head of the Civil Service. Fearful of the knowledge which had been entrusted to me I always insisted on taking William to my club for lunch, and we only parted company when I took my seat in the gallery of the House of Commons to hear the Budget speech.

There were two annual events to which Chancellors went, one was the Commonwealth Finance Ministers' Conference which was always succeeded by a meeting of the World Bank, usually, though not always, held in Washington. I succeeded in persuading Derick Heathcoat Amory that I should be allowed to go to the World Bank meetings and attended my first in New Delhi in 1958. At this meeting Derick had to go home early and the young Reggie Maudling, then Economic Secretary to the Treasury, was left in charge of the British delegation when still in his thirties. He seemed to me brilliant, friendly and lackadaisical. I have always enjoyed meeting him ever since that first encounter though his laissez-faire attitude to Northern Ireland is one of the reasons why the present grave situation has arisen.

Of all the Chancellors I dealt with, Derick Amory was the most charming and Selwyn Lloyd the most helpful. When the Pay Roll Tax was introduced, Northern Ireland went up in smoke. Private assurances to me that it would probably never be used were of no avail because I could not use them in public. When interviewed by the Northern Ireland press, as I emerged from leaving the Budget statement, I made it plain that we could not welcome it and moreover that I would be seeing the Chancellor the following morning. About a month later Selwyn had his officials in to hear my arguments and then asked them to defend its application to Northern Ireland. I could detect that the officials didn't really have their heart in applying the tax to Northern Ireland. After they had left Selwyn assured me that Northern Ireland would be excluded—but the timing must be left to him. In the end we were excluded on the third reading of the Finance Bill, by which time it was too late for Scotland to demand similar treatment!

It so happened that I had a letter from him on the day he was peremptorily sacked by Mr Macmillan. I knew him well enough for him to add a PS saying that this would be his last letter from the Treasury. This, I think, indicates how swiftly and unwisely the 'butcher' acted. In fact I was in his room after Budget day when Mr Macmillan had rung up to complain about the bad reception of the Budget and Selwyn vigorously defended himself. This presumably was the warning a few months before the execution.

When I went to the Ministry of Finance we had no national museums in Northern Ireland. My first effort lay in the direction of a folk museum. Northern Ireland tends to be parochial in its approach to nearly everything and when I was preparing the ground for the acceptance of the idea I was only asked three questions. First, who would be the head of it? Second, how much would he get paid? Third, where would it be situated? How many projects had foundered because of this attitude! My reply was simple. I asked that approval should be given to this idea in principle and that then a committee should be set up to advise us on all these matters. In this way local authorities were unable to fight over its location and MPs were unable to say that they would not support the idea unless so and so got the job of running it. Previous efforts to establish a much smaller institution had all foundered on these points. Today we have a first rate institution on a magnificent site some ten miles from Belfast and the excellent Director, George Thompson, and his wares took part in the British Week in Macy's Store, New York, some three years ago.

Then we moved on to the formation of a National Museum and Art Gallery. In this we were immensely assisted by the charming and sensible chairman of the committee dealing with the Municipal Museum in Belfast, Miss McAlery. She persuaded her committee to ask the Government to take it over. If we had appeared to try and take it over ourselves then municipal pride would have blocked us. Once again, after months of patient work behind the scenes, victory was achieved, and at the time of writing a large extension is nearing completion. Valuable works of art have already been purchased and I hope I shall live to see a fine collection of the little known works of the artists of the Royal Hibernian Academy. This latter institution was formed in the 1830s on the lines of the Royal Academy in London.

While I was Minister an opportunity arose for me to appoint the first Irish head of the Ministry of Finance, Bobs Dunbar. Until then, in a kind of Colonial fashion, it had been thought necessary that the head of the Civil Service should be English or Scottish. Bobs, born and brought up in Dublin, was one of the most popular men in the

Service, and I was delighted to work with him, as I had done previously in Home Affairs. Brought up in the pre-war atmosphere at Stormont, where lack of money and vast unemployment were the order of the day, he was a little given to saving candle ends. One day when the World Bank meeting in New York was approaching and was to be succeeded by an industrial tour of the States—Northern Ireland has more than thirty American factories today—I said to my private secretary, 'Let's ring up Ken Bloomfield in New York to finalise details.' A look of horror spread over Dunbar's face. One could almost read what it said, 'Could Ulster afford a call to New York?' I had nothing but admiration for this man and incidentally he was the best 'trouble-shooter' in the Civil Service. It was tragic that he was killed when driving to a church service in Belfast to be taken by his son-in-law. There was so much he could have done in a small community like Northern Ireland after his retirement.

For years Northern Ireland had had a bad industrial press in London. One would open the *Financial Times* and see a headline 'NEW FACTORY FOR CORK.' Underneath one would see something of the following nature. 'This factory, which is making bed-socks, will, when in full production, expect to employ forty-five people.' At the same moment a new factory to employ 3,000 people in Northern Ireland would not get a mention. Obviously something had to be done about it. At that time the *Belfast Telegraph* had a brilliant political correspondent, Tommy Roberts. I arranged for him to go to the Ulster office in London, despite the opposition of the Cabinet offices in Northern Ireland. Within weeks the situation was transformed. Not only was Tommy known by all the journalists in Fleet Street, and the 'lobby' at Westminster, but at last Northern Ireland was getting good headlines. Recently he has been unwisely withdrawn to Belfast, and Northern Ireland has paid a heavy price. One day I suggested to him that Belfast should figure in the temperature charts as well as Dublin. This was duly arranged and everyone in Britain can now see how hot or cold it was in Belfast on the previous day—unfortunately recently it has tended to be hot!

There has often been talk as to whether or not Northern Ireland was properly treated by the Treasury. I think I can testify to the fact that so long as one had good relations with the officials one was properly treated. During my period at the Ministry of Finance I dealt with five different Chancellors, obviously therefore it was the officials one dealt with and it was doubtful whether the busy Chancellors ever mastered the incredibly complicated financial arrangements which exist between the two departments.

To a large extent Northern Ireland's income rested on attributions of revenue. How, for instance, does one accurately assess Northern Ireland's fair share of the Tobacco Revenue? The answer is that if you put your case well and establish a good rapport you will get a generous attribution. If, on the other hand, you accept a figure worked out by some junior official in the Customs and Excise Department you may get considerably less than your due. It is in these ways that an active Minister of Finance can help.

I remember when I persuaded the Treasury to let us have our own Ulster Development Bonds it was all fixed up without any difficulty. For years previously Northern Ireland people had been investing in National Defence Bonds and the money had been going to London. There were some at Stormont who felt that what was good enough for the good old days was good enough for the 1960s, but I didn't agree. Of course we were lucky in that we were such a small part of the whole that concessions to us were, as I often used to say, 'a drop in the bucket' to Whitehall. In fact I found that the Treasury respected one if one fought one's corner, and certainly I look back on nothing but happy memories of inter-exchequer relations.

One of the drawbacks of one Party rule extending over many years is that MPs tend to think that if only they can rock the boat sufficiently they may then make a place for themselves in the Cabinet. While Cabinet ministers intent on trying to climb the Cabinet ladder feel that if they can have a more senior ministry they may enhance their future prospects. During my time at the Ministry of Finance various attempts were made to unseat me. None is worthy of mention except one which shows up some sections of the Unionist Party in a poor light. I have already explained that the Ministry of Finance was responsible for the Civil Service and consequently for recruiting into it. In a country where there are not many jobs available, the local Civil Service is obviously attractive and I think there is no doubt that Catholic schools encourage their pupils to enter the Service. I was one day made aware that a whispering campaign was afoot. It went as follows. 'Now that there is a liberal minded minister in Finance, Catholics are being encouraged to join the Civil Service and we shall soon be swamped. We must get this stopped now.' Of course anyone who knows how the Civil Service is recruited knows perfectly well that ministers can have no say in who joins the Service and that the administration is carried out by officials, but a sectarian smear is easy to start in Ulster. In the end a Party meeting was held, but fortunately there were enough people of good sense to back me up, and when I suggested that if I resigned I would say why, the whole plot fell to the ground.

Before I reach the period when I moved from Stormont to Stormont Castle I think I should face up to the difficulty of saying a word about my predecessor, Lord Brookeborough. He was a man of immense personal charm. He was good company and a good raconteur and those who met him imagined that he was relaxing away from his desk. What they didn't realise was that there was no desk.

A man of limited intelligence, his strong suits were shooting and fishing in Fermanagh and when he came up on Monday night or Tuesday morning it was difficult to shake him from some of his more idiotic ideas. In short, it would have been quite impossible, even with his immense charm, for him to have been a minister in London.

In February 1963 he had an operation for a duodenal ulcer. This was something which had worried him for many years and political life did not improve it. About a week after his return home I thought I would call down to see him and ran slap into photographers and press leaving the official residence. It seemed incredible but the purpose of the game soon became apparent, it was to show the world that he was all right. 'Wasn't I clever,' Lady Brookeborough said to me, 'I had Basil standing up when they came in, because he finds it very hard to get out of a chair?' But a very high price was soon to be paid for this 'public appearance'.

About a fortnight later my Cabinet colleagues asked me how the Prime Minister was getting on and as I hadn't heard anything about him I again called round at the official residence. A maid who opened the door looked surprised to see me. 'His Lordship is in bed, but you could see her Ladyship.' At this point the astonished reader will ask how it was possible for the Prime Minister of the day to be held incommunicado. I can only reply by saying that during the fifties the Brookeboroughs had spent the whole winter in Australia and New Zealand going each way by ship. Anything was possible in those easy going days.

On being shown in I was told by Lady Brookeborough that I could go and see the Prime Minister—but only for five minutes. Fortunately, after telling me that he felt worse than he had ever done in his many previous duodenal illnesses, he asked me how things were going. I replied that everything was going fine. He seemed surprised, but then we must remember what had happened to him just before his operation. A note was to be handed to him on which was appended ten back-bench signatures out of a Party of about thirty-five members. As soon, however, as the 'rebels' heard that he was going to hospital the note asking for his resignation was immediately withdrawn.

I told him that all would be well till the end of the Easter recess, but that if he stayed away till the autumn—that is, for another six months—things would become impossible. As this was March and the Easter recess would not end till the beginning of May I was suggesting a convalescence of six weeks. He seemed curiously un-interested and I remember thinking that a further journey to Fermanagh during April would be required to impress upon him that he could not stay away for several months.

That afternoon in the House the Chief Whip asked me what arrangements had been made for the Home Secretary's forthcoming visit, and I replied that I had really intended to raise that point myself, but finding the Prime Minister in bed, instead of up and about as I had imagined, I decided I could not bother him with such details. He offered to find out himself, and I warned him that if he telephoned he would merely be told to stay away. In the event Lady Brooke-borough gave him the astonishing intelligence that he needn't worry about the arrangements—'Terence will have him to stay in this house.' We both concluded that my wife and I would have to move into Stormont House in order to entertain the Home Secretary when he came in April, but we were both rather mystified.

The following Sunday the telephone rang. It was Cynthia Brooke-borough. 'Will you both come to lunch?' she said. I explained that Jean, my wife, was going to Rowallane, the National Trust Garden which she looks after, in order to meet and show round a visitor. She replied that we must both come as 'we are going off into space tomorrow'. So after consulting Jean it was agreed that we would both come up to Stormont which is quite close to Rowallane, but that she would leave just before 1 o'clock.

On arrival it was explained to us that Basil had resigned the day before, and that the Governor, Lord Wakehurst, would be sending for me the following evening. Basil seemed better than when I last saw him, and I really felt rather sorry for the old boy. 'We've been going for drives every day,' his wife said, 'in order to get him fit for the long drive down to Fermanagh tomorrow.'

After lunch was over, Basil was sent up for his afternoon rest and I was given a lecture by Cynthia on what I should do. I bore this with patience knowing it was the last lecture I would have. Before leaving I expressed the hope that they would stay on in the house for another month. I based this suggestion on the knowledge that Lord Avon had gone down to Chequers on his retirement. She was delighted and it was agreed that when Henry Brooke, the Home Secretary, came she would be the hostess at Stormont House. From everything that was said I was led to believe that my predecessor had put my name forward to the Governor. Obviously the decision was the Governor's alone, for in those days Unionist Prime Ministers were selected in the same way as their Conservative counterparts in Britain, where the Queen used to send for the person she thought most suitable.

The Attorney General, Edmond Warnock, who had resigned from the Government in 1956, made things as difficult for me as he could for the first four years of my premiership, because he never forgave me for my part in stopping him bringing down the Government in 1956 over the Rent De-restriction Act. Only when he knew that he would not be standing again at the following election did he swing round and support me, much to the fury of the extreme constituency which he represented in Belfast. During that first summer when he was making things hot for me, I ran into Basil Brookeborough at Stormont. He said how sorry he was that I was having trouble with the same people as he had done. I replied that this was inevitable unless I took some of them into the Cabinet. 'Well,' he said, 'it is an attack on me, because you were my choice as my successor.' Only a short time later I was to discover the real story of his resignation from the only man who could know.

It was about six months after I became Prime Minister that the Governor told me how awkward Basil Brookeborough had been at his resignation. Lord Wakehurst had reminded him that as retiring Prime Minister he had a right to suggest the name of his successor, but that he, as Governor had no need to accept it. Brookeborough told Wakehurst that the Home Office had assured him that he need not put any name forward. As Wakehurst was unable to extract any views from his retiring Prime Minister he then told him that he intended to send for me and invited a comment. But he refused to say anything.

When told this story later, I was flabbergasted. Here was a man who had no political future and yet he wanted to ensure that he would have no political trouble in retirement if his successor got into difficulties. My immediate reaction was unfavourable. Since then, however, I have, I think, unravelled the story. At that time he was intending to retire from Stormont altogether, and when his son succeeded he obviously wanted to see him as a minister as soon as possible. If, however, I or any other successor got into serious trouble, he wanted to be able to assure the Unionist Party that the successor was not his choice. This he duly did at the Party meeting in 1966 at the time of the 'conspiracy'.* Meanwhile he had to stay on for five years as a nominal MP before he could feel sure his son would succeed him as the Unionist candidate.

* This event is described later on. It refers to the efforts of certain back-benchers to unseat me in the year when the Dublin Rebellion of 1916 was celebrated in Belfast.

6

 Stormont Castle

I BECAME Prime Minister of Northern Ireland at about 6 p.m. at
Government House, Hillsborough on Monday, 25 March 1963.
The process was quickly over in the Governor's, Lord Wakehurst's study. He then insisted on taking me into the drawing room
where we both had a whisky-and-soda. Realising that there was much
to do I became somewhat restive as time drifted by, but in the end I
got away. As we drove away from the gates of Hillsborough Castle
I turned to my driver, Raymond Hueston, sitting beside me and said,
'I think I ought to tell you that the Governor has asked me to be
Prime Minister.' In a quiet voice he replied, 'I am not in the least
surprised.' Would others, I wondered, as we drove back to Stormont,
take the whole thing for granted? Or would there be trouble during
the next few days? Who could tell? But in any case I had to hurry
on and ring up the members of the Cabinet who I wanted to stay on
in their jobs.

Northern Ireland's provincial government had always been very
much part-time and ministers were allowed to hold directorships.
There was now no point in going back to Stormont as everything,
including the telephone exchange, would be shut. Instead I went to
my private secretary's, Jim Malley's house and got him to act as
telephone operator on his own telephone. We had one or two amusing
incidents. There was a minister called Morgan who I wanted to stay
on in his job where, at that time, he was doing well. There was also
a back-bencher called Morgan who had the same initials reversed. A
call was accidentally put through to the back-bencher's home—mercifully he was out! Lord Glentoran was Leader of the Senate and I
wanted him to stay on in that capacity. Jim rang his home number
and the butler replied: 'No, sir, I am afraid Lord Glentoran is in
his bath.' 'Well,' said Jim, 'could I speak to Lady Glentoran?' 'No,

sir, Lady Glentoran is in her bath too.' Progress in completing the Cabinet was slow!

On the way home I suddenly remembered that I hadn't rung up the Chairman of the Party. I stopped in Belfast and got through to him. Not a word of congratulation, just a long pause and then the question, 'Will there be dissension in the Party?' This was the first chilling remark and I wondered whether he had already known and already been preparing trouble himself—he had an unsympathetic personality. In fact he was proved quite wrong and the following morning—the announcement was released from Government House at 10 p.m. that night—the press was glowing with goodwill. Even more surprising, the Party meeting was the pleasantest that I ever attended before or since and seemed unanimous in confirming my appointment. As I have already explained I was selected in the old Conservative way; nor was I the last Unionist to emerge in this manner—Sir Alec Douglas-Home was to emerge six months later, though because of the manner of Mr Macmillan's going the whole process was so painful that the system then died a natural death, and I think it would be hard to justify in the 1970s. On the other hand, would Pitt or Gladstone or Disraeli have become Prime Minister if there had been a Party vote?

Immediately after the meeting my wife and I had to attend a long-planned lunch for Mr Cecil King, then the boss of the *Daily Mirror* group. Later that summer I paid a return visit to the *Daily Mirror*. I was rather surprised, some while later, to see that Mr King said in an article in *The Times* that he had given me good advice on Irish affairs soon after I had been appointed, and that had I taken it, all would have been well. I have no recollection of advice good or bad on either occasion. At Stormont, my memory is, I found his wife very charming. In London I remember being told how wrong it was of Lord Thomson to acquire the *Belfast Telegraph*, and receiving a diatribe about the iniquities of the Conservative Government in general and Mr Macmillan in particular. All good clean fun perhaps, but certainly not advice on Irish affairs, about which Mr King could hardly have been up to date.

A week after taking over I made an inspection of Stormont Castle. This early Victorian Scottish baronial castle was built by a sinister clergyman called Cleland. He was tutor to Castlereagh whom he saved from drowning in nearby Strangford Lough. Later, in gratitude, the Foreign Secretary presented him with Dundonald, an outlying area of the Londonderry estate. On this land Cleland erected what must originally have been an attractive country house, which was later further castellated in about 1870.

What I discovered was not attractive. Purchased at the time that the Government of Northern Ireland was set up, it was occupied by James Craig, the first Prime Minister of Northern Ireland. At that time the tiny Cabinet Secretariat was housed in the Ballroom and cleared out on the rare occasions that the Cabinet met. From being a country house it was gradually taken over for various official uses during the war. Fortunately a section of the Ministry of Labour had just been moved out before my predecessor retired. But even a look at the rooms occupied by the Cabinet offices was pretty horrifying. After walking up some steps covered by a glass roof reminiscent of a London theatre, one entered a hall where the messengers made their tea, then went on into another hall which looked like a dentist's waiting room with all the stuffing coming out of the chairs. One then clattered on down a brown-linoleum-covered passage past a gurgling lavatory into the Prime Minister's study. All the staff were on the first floor and one's only form of communication was a bell either for a messenger or for the Permanent Secretary. The evidence of its former use as a country house was all too clear and the conditions in which I found a typist working decided me there and then to send for the chief architect to the Ministry of Finance.

Charles Munro was a Scotsman and I had got to know him well in the Works branch of the Ministry of Finance. I had been very keen to stop some of the old buildings in our provincial towns from being pulled down, especially Georgian and early Victorian courthouses which the judiciary would have gladly seen levelled to the ground. I am glad to say I succeeded. Charles was thrilled at being able to get his hands on Stormont Castle. He told me he had been longing to restore it for years. Apart from anything else, he told me, it was an appalling fire risk as it stood at that time. Certainly with electric kettles plugged into what had been bedside lamp sockets I felt he had a good case. Moreover 10 Downing Street had just been completely renovated, one might almost say rebuilt.

On 5 April we had the annual meeting of the Ulster Unionist Council at which I said that the Government's task was to transform the face of Ulster. This was greeted with cheers and I received a standing ovation. How often have I heard the clergy in Ulster preaching in favour of toleration. So long as it is kept in general terms then everyone is happy. If, however, they actually say something specific about welcoming their Catholic neighbours into their homes or their church halls to play bowls, then the trouble really starts. My speech fell into the first category.

My predecessor had been Prime Minister for twenty years. In normal times 73 might have seemed almost past the age of normal retirement, but as Sir Winston Churchill had retired only during the previous decade at the age of 80, it wasn't at that time considered to be a great age. As I see it the tragedy of his premiership was that he did not use his tremendous charm, and his deep Orange roots to try and persuade his devoted followers to accept some reforms. The back-bench reaction to the Education Act, on which I made my maiden speech, was his last act of political courage, and that had been in 1946, seventeen years before. The following year he had sacked his Minister of Education under extremist pressure and ever since then had played safe. In twenty years as Prime Minister he never crossed the border, never visited a Catholic school and was never received or sought a civic reception from a Catholic town.

His latter days were taken up with two pet aversions. First, he was determined never to recognise the trade unions, and second, he condemned planning, which he regarded as a socialist menace. In its leader on 5 April, written the day after the Unionist Conference, the *Belfast Telegraph* said, 'How far the climate has suddenly changed under the new Premier was indicated at yesterday's Party Conference, when delegates refused to pass a motion endorsing the Government's refusal to recognise the Irish Congress of Trade Unions.' Little did that leader writer, doubtless the late lamented Jack Sayers, realise how many months it would take me to get the Party to accept recognition.

A month after becoming Prime Minister I called on Mr Macmillan at Admiralty House. No satirical writer could have improved on the occasion. On being shown into the Cabinet Room I espied the Prime Minister standing at a dumb waiter apparently reading a book—Trollope presumably. Turning slowly round he expressed feigned surprise at my arrival. 'Hallo, my dear boy, come and sit down.' He expressed the hope that things would turn out well and then added, 'I thought Brooke stayed on much too long.' He was, however, surprised that I wanted to talk about anything other than the weather, though he volunteered the information that everything was going his way and that at the next election he would benefit from the present situation. Years later at lunch at Downing Street with Mr Wilson I mentioned that I had gone to Admiralty House in April 1963. 'Oh,' he replied reflectively, from his photographic memory, 'that was when I first heard about Profumo.' History was to show that everything was not going Macmillan's way at that particular time.

Macmillan also told me a story which I thought in questionable taste, even if it were true. President Kennedy, on his recent European trip, had stopped at Chatsworth to see his sister's, Lady Hartington's, grave, and the Prime Minister had arranged that he should also be shown the grave of Lord Frederick Cavendish, who had been murdered in Phoenix Park, Dublin, by the Fenians. This was, of course, a foul murder and the Kennedys are of Irish descent, but I doubt whether it would have had the slightest effect on the President if serious trouble had erupted in Ireland in his day. It certainly did not deter me from pursuing my main objective at that meeting.

When we had run out of small talk I said I had a proposition to make. 'Would it be possible,' I asked, 'for President Kennedy to visit and open the Giant's Causeway on his way back from his European tour while on his way to Dublin?' He looked surprised. I continued. 'The RAF tell me that the presidential jet could be landed at Bally-kelly aerodrome, from where a few minutes would bring him to the Giant's Causeway in a helicopter. The whole operation would only take three hours.' Still musing he asked why I wanted to make myself unpopular with the Ulster Protestants. I replied that I thought that by honouring an Irish-American president we might bring both sides together and that I knew from frequent visits to America that the vast numbers of Irish-Americans hated Britain and that perhaps this would help London as well. He then waved a languid hand in the direction of Tim Bligh, his Private Secretary. 'You might get on to David* in Washington,' he said.

I was later to learn from David Ormsby-Gore that this was the wrong way to go about things, but as a new boy I thought I ought to 'follow the book'. I wish now I had made an approach to the ambassador first, but unfortunately although we were at the same school, we were there at different times, nor had I met him during the War. I am sure that had I known him at that time I would have made an attempt to get Washington reaction first.

Apart from the lateness of the invitation, made when his itinerary had already been announced, I fear that the Democratic Party, which gets the Irish vote in America, must have discouraged such a visit. However, he sent me a charming personal note through the American Consul General in Belfast and I wrote and thanked him for it.

In this letter I had told him the story about my lunch with the Scotch-Irish Society of Philadelphia some years previously. On this

* Sir David Ormsby-Gore, later Lord Harlech.

occasion an elderly millionaire wrote on a piece of paper all the American millionaires whom he knew to be of Scotch-Irish, or Ulster Presbyterian, descent. When I had read it he said, 'So you see, Captain, the Scotch-Irish own America.' And then as a tear coursed down his cheek, he added, 'But I'm afraid the Southern Irish run it.' I added for good measure that this was before Kennedy's inauguration! I think he enjoyed this story. In any case, I had a very nice reply and I feel in all the circumstances that I should print it in full.

Dear Mr Prime Minister:

Thank you for your thoughtful personal letter of May 6th, and for the spirit in which you have accepted my message about the Giant's Causeway. I fully understood the personal warmth of your invitation, and I am genuinely sorry that my schedule simply leaves no room for this stop in June.

I am much interested to know of your efforts on behalf of the homes of American Presidents of Scotch-Irish descent, and I am sure that Mrs Kennedy would enjoy having the photographs of which you speak.

I hardly dare to comment on your amusing story about the relationship between the Scotch-Irish and the Southern Irish in the United States because it would seem unwise to transfer arguments about the ownership of Ireland to the larger area of this country, but I will say that we take pride in all the good Americans that have come out of all parts of Ireland and are grateful to you for your interest in this relationship. The next time you come to Washington, I hope you will let me know so that we can meet and have a talk. Meanwhile, I thank you again for your friendly letter.

Sincerely,
John Kennedy

My first troubles at home were to come with my insistence that there should be a Code of Conduct for Cabinet ministers. Ever since the Northern Ireland Government had been set up it had been the practice for Ministers to work part-time. I remember Lord Brookeborough himself telling me that when he had been made Minister of Agriculture before the War he had been told that one afternoon a week would suffice for the discharge of his duties. Earlier in the year there had been a row over a nominal directorship held by Lord Glentoran, the Leader of the Senate, so I was quite determined that something should be officially laid down. Under the new rules it would still be possible for ministers to hold compatible directorships, but even the following sentence, 'a minister should avoid any outside interest which makes such demands upon his time and energies that it becomes difficult for him properly to discharge the prior responsibilities of his Public Office', was received with less than a welcome by some of my colleagues.

I was probably in the fortunate position of being the only member of the Cabinet who had no business interests, so obviously I could not expect the proposals to be received with enthusiasm. But I was soon informed that three or four of my colleagues had been seen discussing this matter in the dining room and hints were made to me that my predecessor, whose son had business interests, would never have agreed to these measures. However, I ploughed on with my ideas and announced the new Code of Conduct in reply to a question. The press was universal in its commendation and I smiled when I read at the end of one leader, 'the Cabinet are to be congratulated for acting with that decisiveness which was lacking when the issue was last raised in the House'.

This first summer also saw the death of Pope John. I sent a published note of condolence to Cardinal Conway at Armagh and the astonished people of Belfast saw a headline which read: 'THE POPE: ULSTER PREMIER'S MESSAGE.' Moreover, this was only one month before 12 July, a date unknown to the average Englishman, but the day of the great Protestant parade in Ulster. The *Irish Times* pointed out that when the Irish Cardinal's predecessor had died earlier in the year my predecessor had only thought it prudent to communicate with a Nationalist MP at Stormont. Moreover, taking a lead from the general atmosphere the Lord Mayor of Belfast had the flag over the City Hall flown at half mast.

As is usual in Northern Ireland, Stormont rose before 12 July and on the whole the press seemed pleased with what had been achieved in fifteen weeks. One paper's headline reviewing the period read: 'Premiership is born,' the other: 'New Leaders ready to meet challenge.' Little did these two political correspondents realise how difficult it had been to change direction. It is one thing for Mr Macmillan to talk of a wind of change blowing on another Continent; but a very different matter when you have to initiate the change yourself and try to drag behind you a reactionary and reluctant Party which has been in power since 1921. Planning was a dirty word. Assurances had been given that the Northern Committee of the Irish Congress of

Trade Unions would not be recognised, even though the British trade unions in the Province belonged to it. And finally the most farcical of all situations: even though the Speaker had recognised the small Northern Ireland Labour Party as the official Opposition, the Government refused to do so, despite the fact that the Nationalist Party declined to constitute themselves into an official Opposition. But while I might have won the support of the press I had already driven the first right-wing nail into my coffin.

Towards the end of September I set out for a North American visit, flying first to Ottawa where one of my former Chancellors, Derick Heathcoat Amory, was now High Commissioner. Changing planes at Montreal we arrived at Earnscliffe, the official residence in Ottawa, just in time for a dinner party. The next day I lunched with the Canadian Prime Minister, Mr Lester Pearson, whom I had met in London earlier in the summer. We compared notes between the difficulties in Canada and Northern Ireland and came to the conclusion that there were undoubtedly some similarities.

From Ottawa we went on to Washington. This time I had let the Ambassador know that I was coming to attend the World Bank meeting for the last time, as the new Minister of Finance was not keen to go and I was determined not to let this Treasury concession drop. I told him that the President had asked me to let him know when I was in Washington in his personal letter received in May, and that this time I would leave all arrangements in his hands. On arrival I went to see David Ormsby-Gore. He said he had been on to the White House, but that the omens did not look good. However, as an alternative he had arranged for us to go to lunch with Bobby Kennedy. I had, in fact, known all this before I left Belfast and we had selected the guests for the Attorney General's lunch before we left Belfast, but I had still hoped that perhaps a short visit to the White House might be arranged—but it was not to be. Everyone was disappointed, including McGeorge Bundy, the President's aide who sat next to my wife at an Embassy dinner a few days later. Once again I heard the full story a little later!

The lunch held in the suite next to the Attorney General's office was fascinating. First I was shown his various children's drawings on the walls of his office, then we went into lunch. A congressman who was to sit on my left had not arrived so Bobby had his place cleared away. As soon as this had been achieved he arrived and the place had to be relaid. The second course was slow in coming so he charged into the kitchen to see why it wasn't ready. During the passage of our lunch I explained to him that we gave substantial grants to Roman Catholic schools and virtually paid 100 per cent of their running expenses. He was dumbfounded. 'Is it not against your constitution?' he said. I doubt whether he really believed what I had told him! Towards the end of the meal a secretary came and dropped a piece of paper in his lap; guessing that something had happened, I said, 'If you have a problem please don't worry about me, you have kindly invited all the people I wanted to meet in Washington and I can stay on and talk to them.' He came out of his thoughts and said to me, 'Jack wants me in the White House right now and I've got to fly to California.' He turned to the girl who was waiting— 'Would you tell the President I've just got to go to California.'

He was the nearest thing I have ever met to a human dynamo, not attractive but very interesting. I was glad to meet him, but sorry not to meet his brother. However, before we left David Ormsby-Gore assured me that next time I came to Washington we would definitely go to the White House. He had told me earlier that the President had sounded rather embarrassed when he had told him that I was coming to Washington, and he knew he would like to meet me. Little did either of us know at that time that fate would decree otherwise.

On our return to Belfast we were faced with the opening of a new session and the preparation of the Queen's Speech. Traditionally this is one of the more important occasions for the Prime Minister makes a big speech on the first day of the Queen's Speech debate. I had by now persuaded my colleagues that we must have an Economic Plan for Northern Ireland and that Professor Tom Wilson of Glasgow University, himself an Ulsterman, was the person to produce it. We were still in difficulties over the setting up of an Economic Council because the Parliamentary Party, ably assisted by at least one of my colleagues, still refused to recognise the Trade Unions. However, even here we were hopeful of a solution, for behind the scenes discussions were continuing with the Trade Unions.

However the Speech itself went like a bomb. Headlines like 'O'NEILL BLUEPRINT FOR ULSTER', 'LABOUR THUNDER STOLEN' and 'PATTERN FOR PROSPERITY' were to be seen on every hand. While an anonymous letter apparently written by the former Attorney General, Edmond Warnock, questioning my right to be Prime Minister was dished out to back-benchers in the wake of the extraordinary scenes at the Tory Conference after Mr Macmillan's retirement. It turned out to be a damp squib but was indicative of how the right wing were not willing to accept change and still yearned for the good old days.

November 22 was a day I shall always remember. I went to visit the new Prime Minister, Sir Alec Douglas-Home, at 10 Downing Street. My reception was as different from the visit to Admiralty House as chalk from cheese. I was immediately made to feel welcome and when, for instance, I suggested that the new carrier then being planned for the Navy should be built at Harland & Woolf, a note was made of this suggestion. During the discussion it emerged that he had got to know Mr Lemass (Prime Minister of the Irish Republic) when he was at the Commonwealth Office and he expressed the hope that I would be able to meet him at some suitable date, a sentiment with which I wholeheartedly agreed. After the meeting we went and had a family lunch upstairs and Jean joined us for the occasion. It was all so friendly and informal that one found it hard to believe. It was immediately agreed that he and Elizabeth Douglas-Home would visit Ulster in the New Year. I left feeling that I had a friend at Court if ever we should need special assistance.

That evening a reception was given by the London Ulster Association in our honour and as we were leaving the Overseas League the hall porter said there was a rumour that President Kennedy had been shot at and wounded. I was going on to have dinner with Joe Garner, the head of the Commonwealth Office, at my club and when I got there the hall porter told me the President was dead. Joe and I were gloomy at that meal, but before it started I rang up and dictated a telegram of sympathy to Bobby Kennedy. I would never meet Jack Kennedy now.

The following week we adjourned both Houses of Parliament as a mark of respect, but not before we had paid our tribute. In my remarks to the House I described the President as master of the spoken word, who was able in the full majesty of the English language to lead the West along the paths of peace as once Sir Winston led them to victory. 'Wherever youth and gaiety are admired, and forward looking and enlightened policies are valued, he will be missed and mourned,' I concluded.

It was not long before I received a black-edged card from Bobby Kennedy enclosing a photograph of his brother. It read as follows:

Dear Prime Minister:
My deep appreciation for your message at the time of the death of my brother—I was very grateful to hear from you.
Bob Kennedy

7
1964

MARCH 1964 turned out to be quite an eventful month. Before it ended I would have completed my first year as Prime Minister. During the first week Sir Alec Douglas-Home flew into Sydenham Airport from London. Sydenham is beside the Shorts aircraft factory, and accompanied by Lady Douglas-Home he was to tour the factory before a Unionist lunch. Shorts' two aircraft were awaiting his inspection: the Belfast freighter and the Skyvan.

All day and everywhere his charm was much to the fore. At lunch in the Ulster Hall, which was packed for the occasion, I presented him with an Ulster tie (the Red Hand is its foundation!) and he immediately tore off his MCC tie and replaced it with this new one. That afternoon we took him round Harland & Wolff, our vast shipyard, which duly impressed him. As is usual on these occasions, he was presented with a blackthorne stick. One small incident still remains in my memory from that afternoon. As we went through a line of workmen in one of the vast 'shops' someone shouted in reply to the Prime Minister's friendly wave—'No surrender.' Alec asked me what he had said and so I tried a 'potted' explanation of 'No surrender'! But he was understandably quite unable to comprehend and in the end his attention was directed somewhere else. This small incident is yet another example of the gulf between the average British person and the average Ulsterman. What the Ulsterman imagines to be common knowledge to the British person is, in fact, unintelligible to him, except perhaps in certain parts of Glasgow and Liverpool.

That night we had a very pleasant dinner in the Great Hall at Stormont. At the top table we had Dennis Taylor, Shorts' chief test pilot, who had shown Alec over the Belfast freighter that morning; and Paddy Hopkirk who had just won the Monte Carlo rally in a Mini Cooper. It was one of the most pleasant occasions which I remember.

54

The following morning I drove the Prime Minister down to Green-mount Agricultural College near Antrim. As we drove through Belfast he suddenly said, 'How did you get on with your motorways?' That, indeed, raised a recent memory! Bill Craig, now famous for his extreme views, was as keen as I was to improve the infra-structure of the Province when in the Cabinet. During the winter it appeared that the Treasury were going to cut down on his motorway building programme. I realised that John Boyd Carpenter, who had been made First Secretary to the Treasury, had the specific job of curtailing expenditure. He was also a member of the Cabinet. It would have been pointless for the Minister of Finance to visit the Chancellor. In all the circumstances I decided to use the friendship I had struck up with the Prime Minister. I went to No 10. When I arrived I was horrified to see Boyd Carpenter already there waiting for me. After a time we were both shown in. John Boyd Carpenter played his cards with great shrewdness. When he thought the Prime Minister, now a Scottish MP, was going to be too helpful, he suddenly observed, 'Of course, you know, Prime Minister, there are no motorways yet in Scotland.' I thought I was now scuppered, but Alec's summing up was masterful. It went something like this. 'The Treasury, rightly or wrongly, agreed to Northern Ireland's motorway programme. I appreciate that we are making all the economies we can, but I cannot agree to this programme being halted. It will continue, but at a slower rate.' I was happy to accept this compromise, I doubt whether the Treasury were pleased!

As we left Belfast he suddenly said. 'Do you know Violet Bonham Carter?' 'Yes,' I replied, 'she is one of my oldest friends.' He then asked me whether I thought she was too old to go to the Lords. My reply was that she should go there as soon as possible. He seemed to agree. Obviously someone, somewhere stopped it. Later, Harold Wilson ensured that Asquith's daughter sat in the Upper House. I am sorry to think that Harold Macmillan, who first created life peers, did not show greater imagination. It is a tragedy that she did not have more time at Westminster.

After leaving Antrim we called at Government House on our way back to Stormont. As we drove down our first motorway from Lisburn back to Belfast we hardly saw a car. I wondered whether he noticed, in any case, he was much too diplomatic to comment! After lunch at Stormont House with several guests, they both left for Scotland. The visit was judged on all sides to be a great success. 'There is no doubt that close up Sir Alec Douglas-Home gives a more pleasing impression

55

than most politicians. The fourteenth Earl of Home would hardly have changed his tie in public, but his "alter ego" did it with complete and fetching aplomb.' So said the *Belfast Telegraph* that evening, in a leader entitled 'Sir Alec at first hand'.

The Prime Ministerial visit was followed by our visit to Cardiff where we had a civic reception in Cardiff Castle. I had already learnt from various functions I had attended that one toasted 'The Queen, Duke of Lancaster in Lancashire' and 'The Queen, Duchess of Normandy in Jersey', but I still remember how horrified the Lord Mayor of Cardiff looked when we both nearly sat down after the National Anthem, without waiting for 'Land of my fathers'! He was a boiler-maker and Ted Hill of the Trades Union movement was spending the night at the Mansion House. Ken Bloomfield and I watched the TV news with Hill that evening while Jean started to change for a dinner. The following morning as we had both enjoyed our crack with him the night before, Ken asked the housekeeper whether we would have the pleasure of Mr Hill's company for breakfast. 'Good heavens, no', she replied, in her charming Welsh accent. 'When Mr Hill comes here we call him in the morning with a pot of tea and half a bottle of whisky and we don't expect to see him till lunchtime!'

In Toronto there is an ancient society known as the 'St Patrick's Protestant Benevolent Society'. Formed at the start of the last century it was supposed to help Irish Protestants who might be in need. Today, with large funds to spare, it gives large functions. I was invited to be their guest for St Patrick's Day, 17 March. As soon as I had accepted I wrote to Lord Harlech in Washington and asked him whether there would be any chance of a visit to the White House. To my great pleasure he advised me to come.

On Sunday, 15 March I flew out to Washington. When I arrived at the Embassy I was shown into a room where David Harlech and Robert Carr were watching television. 'You're just in time,' they said, 'the President [Johnson] is to make his first appearance being questioned by some journalists.' It was fascinating to watch and at the end we all agreed that he had acquitted himself well. This was high praise from Lord Harlech, one of President Kennedy's best friends. When it was over the Ambassador had to go out to dinner and Robert Carr and I had a cold supper together. I found this future Cabinet minister most sympathetic. 'I gather,' he said, 'you had bad luck on your visit last autumn.' 'Yes,' I replied. 'I understand that Lemass's visit to Washington coming just after yours made it difficult for President Kennedy to receive you,' he continued. So there it was. I suppose it was foolish of me not to have realised that before.

The following morning a call was put through to the White House. McGeorge Bundy did not sound encouraging about a morning visit, but thought the afternoon was a possibility. Meanwhile I was told that the Ambassador would take me to see Mrs Kennedy in Georgetown after lunch. Willis Armstrong, an old friend from the State Department, called round to see me, and when I showed him the present I had brought for the President, an album depicting the Ulster, or Scotch Irish, contribution to American history, he said he felt sure the Secretary of State, Dean Rusk, of Scotch Irish descent, would also like to have one.

The following morning I was flying off to Toronto, so it seemed to me that somehow I would have to go to the White House that day, but at lunchtime a message arrived asking me to be at McGeorge Bundy's office the following day at 9 a.m. I protested to David that the Southern Irish would be flaming mad if I were received on St Patrick's Day. However, he pointed out that the new President would hardly be interested in such parochial matters!

I lunched alone with David, and I remember asking him whether it was true that relations between the President and Bobby Kennedy were bad. He told me that he didn't think they had spoken to each other since the assassination, and he doubted whether Bobby Kennedy would stay in the Cabinet much longer.

After lunch he took me to see Jacqueline Kennedy. There were hordes of ladies standing outside the Georgian House and it was with difficulty that the Embassy Rolls nosed its way near the pavement. Two secret servicemen escorted us up the steps and we were shown into a room with windows looking on to the back garden. Even here a secret serviceman walked across that side of the house every ten minutes. The children, who were attending a private school at the British Embassy, had to fight their way in and out of the House and obviously life was already becoming impossible. Soon after, she understandably left for New York.

I found her far more attractive than she appeared in her photographs. Her eyes, which seem too far apart in photographs, look quite natural in real life. David, who, of course, knew her very well, soon started to rag her about some new American financial scandal. I soon found myself joining in and suggested that we were just as bad ourselves in Georgian days. When asked for an example, I cited Lord Holland, who it was alleged had made a fortune out of not paying the troops until a year after their money was due. 'Was that,' she chipped in, 'Charles James Fox's father?' 'Yes,' I replied. 'Oh, I'll forgive him anything.' I wonder how many English girls would have been as quick on the draw?

Cecil Bateman, Secretary to the Cabinet, and I arrived at the White House in good time the following morning and we chatted to Bundy. A call was put through to Kenneth O'Donnell in the President's office, but the President was still at an important breakfast. So in the end we went up to O'Donnell's office. Kennedy's former Private Secretary was celebrating St Patrick's Day by being dressed in green from head to foot. I seem to recall that even his shoes were green. While we waited Pierre Salinger, the Press Secretary, wandered in. I congratulated him on the President's TV appearance, and he told me it was a calculated risk that just had to be taken because of the impending election. While talking to him I became aware that O'Donnell was in difficulties with a new problem, and before long, with or without O'Donnell's permission, someone strode into the President's study. Soon angry voices could be heard coming through the door. The intruder was Senator Mike Mansfield and a further ten minutes elapsed before we were shown in. There, standing behind his desk, black with rage, was the President. I waited near the door for a time until I felt the storm subsiding and then I advanced, gifts under my arm, to shake his hand. I told him I had just arrived at the Embassy in time to see his whole TV appearance and that it was excellent. He then calmed down and led me to the other end of the Presidential study. I was seated on a long sofa and he sat on a rocking chair. I remember asking him whether he was of Scottish or of Scotch Irish descent, but the question was side-stepped! I can't pretend that I found him a sympathetic character. He could so well have kept me waiting another two minutes until he had regained his composure. On the other hand, as the photographic record shows, he was in very good form some fifteen minutes later when the White House photographer came in to take a photograph. I left bitterly regretting that I had not met Jack Kennedy. I felt I was, in a sense, a bit of unfinished business in so far as the Kennedy régime was concerned. 'Do you remember the Giants' Causeway invitation?' said Bundy, as he took me into O'Donnell's room.

Years later in London I heard an amusing tailpiece to my White House visit. An hour after I left the Ambassador from Dublin was shown into O'Donnell's room grasping a large bowl of shamrock for the President. 'You are not,' said O'Donnell, 'the first Irishman to see the President this St Patrick's Day.' The Ambassador looked astonished. 'Captain O'Neill has just left.' The Ambassador nearly dropped his bowl with this piece of shock news! I don't somehow feel that either of the Kennedy brothers would have handled matters in this way. But to Johnson, Bundy, and even our Ambassador, it meant nothing. I can't quite see St Patrick's Day being celebrated in Texas. For me March had been an eventful month.

On 24 April, just over a year after I had become Prime Minister, I took my first step in the direction of improving community relations. I visited a Catholic school in Ballymoney, County Antrim. And what was more, it emerged quite naturally as a result of my known wishes and attitudes. I was making one of my 'meet the people' tours and this visit was included in the schedule. Of course it stole the headlines. The Chairman of the Board of Governors, Canon Clenaghan, had been padre to the Connaught Rangers in the First World War. He gave me a particularly warm welcome, and this was reflected throughout the school. The only thing which I could see which differentiated it from a state school, attended by Protestant children, was a crucifix in the Hall, and thereby hangs a tale. A Belfast paper told one of its photographers to try and get a 'shocking' picture of me during this first ever visit by a Prime Minister of Northern Ireland to a Catholic school. The photographer waited outside the front door and when, an hour later, I emerged, with the aid of his telescopic lens, he made it look as if the crucifix was over my head. I was later shown how Paisley was able to make use of this picture in his own paper. Years later the photographer told me that when he arrived he was horrified to find that there were no nuns or other equally 'shocking' people to greet me and then he suddenly saw the crucifix and realised that his finest hour had arrived. In such ways was co-operation made almost impossible. In such ways reconciliation was bound to fail. It did. As in so much else in Northern Ireland, this story can hardly be comprehensible in England.

The beginning of May saw me spending the night at 10 Downing Street. Both Alec Douglas-Home and I had been at the same House at Eton, the aforementioned A. W. Whitworth, though he was there twelve years before me.

I arrived at tea-time and after being given tea by David Douglas-Home, with the aid of an electric kettle, his mother Elizabeth, returned from some function. The Prime Minister himself popped in to say there was an emergency Cabinet meeting on the South Arabian Federation and urged us all to have a drink. As the Cabinet meeting was at the House, we first of all went down and strolled in the garden and then inspected the Cabinet Room. Finally we returned to the flat for a drink.

Elizabeth seemed a little depressed and so I lifted my glass and said, 'To the next election.' She seemed to be wondering whether they had done the right thing in taking on the premiership, renouncing the peerage, etc. So I simply said, 'To be Prime Minister of the United Kingdom, even for one year, is not given to many people.'

Driving to the dinner at the Hyde Park Hotel we exercised the Prime Minister's right to drive through Horse Guards Arch—the only time I have ever driven through it. On the way to the hotel I asked him whether foreign bases were really worthwhile. 'I'm not sure,' he replied. 'But I am sure of one thing, we should have made friends with Nasser—we've made a mess of Egypt, I'm afraid.'

The Whitworth dinner was fun, but as the people present were all of Alec's vintage I was a little out of my depth. The only person I recognised was John Gladstone, whose two younger brothers, David and Jim, had been both at West Downs and Eton with me. I sat on Whitworth's left and Alec on his right, while John Foster, who had organised the dinner, sat on my left. It started with m'tutor reading 'Absence' and all the 'boys' present answering to their names —there were many interruptions! One story from that evening is worth recalling. John Foster retailed how soon after David Ormsby-Gore had gone to Eton someone at his house (not Whitworth's) had committed suicide. The harassed housemaster assembled all the boys together and asked them if anyone could tell him why this boy had committed suicide. There was a long pause and then this new boy— later to be our Ambassador in Washington—put up his hand. 'Could it,' he spoke hesitantly, 'could it have been because of your food, sir?'

In the morning I left No 10 and was told to come again whenever I wanted a bed, but the tenant of No 10 was to move out himself in October.

A fortnight later my mother's twin sisters, Celia Milnes-Coates and Cynthia Colville, had their eightieth birthday and a party was given for them by their children at the same room in the Hyde Park Hotel. It was a wonderful occasion, slightly marred by my cousin, David Colville, asking me, at the last moment, to propose their healths. As our Aunt Celia always had the most wonderful food at her home at Helperby in Yorkshire, I was able to use to good effect the Eton story, adding that no one was likely to commit suicide because of the food at Helperby. Aunt Cynthia Colville, for many years a lady-in-waiting to Queen Mary, and among other things a social worker in the East end of London, could have played a notable part in politics, like Violet Bonham Carter, had she been free to do so.

That my efforts and activities were not entirely lost south of the border was made evident at this time by a split in the Fine Gael Party in Dublin. The 'city group', consisting largely of businessmen, was expelled from the Party for recognising the Constitution of Northern Ireland. Today's extremists like Bill Craig and John Taylor played a large part in bringing this situation about by their friendship with this section of the Fine Gael Party. The chairman of this branch of that Party ended a statement he issued at that time by saying, 'Captain O'Neill is proving a kindly and courteous leader by endeavouring to meet all the people of the area. He is making visits to Roman Catholic places in which Lord Brookeborough would not have been found dead. No doubt the extreme Unionists are accusing their Prime Minister of "capitulation".'

Northern Ireland now held its first 'party' in London. We had a reception at Claridges. It was a success. Two pickets appeared but got bored and left before the guests departed. Today the hotel would be blown up if any such function were to be held.

Towards the end of July I announced a Cabinet reshuffle. The interesting point about these changes was that they were the first major alterations to the structure of the Government since its inception. In brief, a Ministry of Development comprising the entire infra-structure of the Province was created and a Ministry of Health and Social Services. This latter consisted of the Health side of the old Ministry of Health and Local Government joined to the entire Ministry of Labour.

Three days later I called on Harold Wilson at his room in the House of Commons and among other things we discussed these recent Government changes. I told him that I would really have liked to have called the second new Ministry 'Social Services', but so many people had objected to the omission of the word 'Health' that I had had to agree to this more cumbersome title. He listened to all this with great interest and said he felt there was a pointer in all this for his Party. According to the note I made soon after this meeting, I see that I wrote, 'he is only five days ahead of *The Economist* who really write in glowing terms about the Government changes'. Later I watched with interest the administrative changes which were made by the Labour Government and I smiled when I saw a Ministry of Social Security emerging. At the time of writing these two new

Ministries are still in existence, so they seem to have stood the test of time.

To return to my notes, I feel I ought to print an extract as it may prove of interest to those who have never met the Leader of the Labour Party. 'Call to see Harold Wilson at his room at the House of Commons. I fully expect to dislike him, but instead I find a lot of charm as well as the expected intelligence.' At the end of my notes I say, 'When I tell him how well we were treated by the last Labour Government, he assures me we shall be equally well treated by the next. In fact I enjoy my interview very much indeed and feel that if he wins we shall get on well—I hope I am right.' And so it turned out to be. Harold Macmillan was not my cup of tea. Alec Douglas-Home was everybody's cup of tea. Harold Wilson was detested by many people and quite acceptable to others. I fell into the second category and would add that I think in many ways his public image does not do justice to the real man. The expert image-maker is unable to project himself. Though I must confess that the public opinion polls about his personal popularity do not support my thesis.

From Westminster I went on to a small lunch given for me by Sir Francis Evans (Ulster Agent in London) at the Café Royal. I sat beside Sir Saville—Joe—Garner (Head of Commonwealth Office). Once again I quote from my notes even though, perhaps, remarks made in 1964 do not fully stand the test of time. 'J. G. confirms that the Commonwealth PMs' Conference was a great success for Alec. Indeed he admits that he strongly advised against having one at all on the grounds that Southern Rhodesia and its problems might well wreck the Conference itself, and even unbalance the whole Commonwealth. Though often critical of civil servants, I must confess that I would probably have given the same advice had I been in his shoes. Instead, the Conference has not only improved the PM's standing, but also the prestige of Britain and the Commonwealth. It has certainly rendered null and void the remark in *The Times* this year that the Commonwealth is a "gigantic farce". However time may have altered the course of events, the long-forgotten results of that Conference are a tribute to Alec Douglas-Home's diplomacy. Perhaps a man with a more intellectual approach, or greater political agility, might have failed on this occasion.'

At the end of August the results of eighteen months of behind-the-scenes activity came to an end. We were finally able to achieve recognition of the North Ireland Committee of the Irish Congress of Trades Unions. The donkey work had been carried out by Cecil Bateman,

Secretary to the Cabinet, and Norman Kennedy of the Congress. At last it was possible for the Government to recognise the co-ordinating committee which the British Trade Unions had themselves adopted. Looking back I would say that this was probably one of the most difficult hurdles I surmounted during my premiership. The whole idiotic issue has long been forgotten. At the crucial Party meeting where the matter was settled, Brian Faulkner, who had publicly stated that his relations as Minister of Commerce with individual Unions was excellent, tried to have the decision postponed. Fortunately a Trade Unionist, Senator McGladdery, was listened to with interest, and the small gathering—many MPs were too frightened to attend it—endorsed the Cabinet's decision.

A European trip followed and included a visit to the Ten Horn family at Sionsweg 3, Nijmegen. It was a very happy occasion. Jean was taken up to see the room where I had spent a week in bed after a small wound. It was decorated with orange flowers for Holland. This Catholic family had no idea what 'Orange' meant in Northern Ireland!

In October the Conservatives called their election. During the election a Republican HQ was set up in Divis Street and a tricolour, the Irish Republican flag, was displayed in the window. It sat there for many days unnoticed. Then Paisley stirred up trouble about its presence. Before long the police thought it wise to try and have it removed peacefully. This was not possible, so it had to be removed by force. Rioting ensued—mild by present day standards—but it was unpleasant while it lasted. This is what I said when I spoke in Parliament at Stormont:

Those of us responsible for the Industrial Development of the Province can only deplore the world-wide publicity being given to events of this character when we have laboured to convince the world that Ulster is an ideal place in which to build a factory and give employment to our people.

We cannot go back to the 1920s and 1930s when 100,000 unemployed were the order of the day and misery and privation stalked the streets of Belfast.

I pray God that as we advance in wealth and education and maturity the dreadful scenes which we witnessed will never be repeated, and I trust that men of goodwill throughout our Province will work to that end.

What I really had in mind, at that time, was that there had been sectarian riots in the mid-thirties and I hoped that we were not going to return to those days. In fact, it was not till August 1969 that those days returned, and ensured, among other things, that industrial development would be penalised.

At the end of October our first Ulster Week was held. Nottingham was the venue. Thanks to the wonderful help from everyone in Nottingham, not least the Chamber of Commerce, the venture was a roaring success. The whole city was plastered with Red Hands. The *Belfast News Letter* went mad with excitement over the event the following morning, but a more sober estimate of this new commercial enterprise appeared in one small column of the *Belfast Telegraph* that evening, it read:

> The Prime Minister, Captain Terence O'Neill, launched the Week at a civic luncheon in the Council House.
>
> Shops all over Nottingham had signs proclaiming the event, and Ulster flags were on display in all shops.
>
> Among products of Northern Ireland on which attention is being focused are linen, whiskey, shoes, food, tweeds, heaters, tape recorders and cutlery.
>
> Thousands of Nottingham people turned out to see the Premier.
>
> Captain O'Neill made a tour of local shops, and was interviewed on television. Then he had lunch with the Lord Mayor.
>
> The Week will go on until Friday, ending with a Government reception in the County Hall, West Bridgeford.

In those days the Ulster flag was viewed with suspicion by extreme Protestants. To them the Union Jack was the real Protestant flag. Today, as they become more and more angry with Britain, they are clinging to the Red Hand as something different both from the Union Jack and from the shamrock or the Tricolour. What odd tricks history plays!

On my return from Nottingham we had a visit from General Lemnitzer, who was then in command of SHAPE (Supreme Headquarters Allied Powers Europe) in Paris. The Government gave a dinner for him in the Great Hall at Stormont. I soon discovered that he had a great admiration for President Kennedy and that he was with him during the fateful Cuba crisis. He told me how nice he was to work for and he gave me the impression that he regarded him as a complete gentleman. At one point in the discussions I mentioned the fact that one of Kennedy's chief campaign points had been the missile gap, but that we had not heard much about that after the campaign was over. His face immediately lit up and he dilated on this particular subject. He explained to me that Kennedy had genuinely believed as a Senator (and with all the assistance from the Democratic Party) that there really was a serious missile gap. He inferred that the Russian decision to concentrate on a powerful propellent for the rocket as opposed to the development of a more powerful warhead was well known to the Pentagon and the American decision to concentrate on the warhead as opposed to the propellent was a calculated decision. Indeed, I myself suggested the phrase 'calculated decision', and he readily agreed to it.

Apparently Kennedy's amazement, when told by the Pentagon chiefs that there was, in fact, no missile gap, had to be seen to be believed. It took him some time to recover from the fact that one of his chief campaign issues was, in fact, false, and Lemnitzer had the greatest admiration for the way in which he dealt with the subject, never trying to blame anybody else for what had happened and dealing with the problem as best he could when questioned in public.

The General brought with him, as one of his ADCs, Colonel Crockett. When I met the General at the airport and was introduced to Crockett I immediately asked him whether he was any relation to that famous Scotch-Irishman, Davy Crockett. He told me that five generations back his forebear had been Davy Crockett's brother.

Meeting Lemnitzer was a charming interlude. He struck me as extremely youthful for someone who had been at West Point in the First World War. He had a wonderful sense of humour and gaiety. After the dinner was over he enjoyed seeing the Senate Chamber and the House of Commons and much enjoyed sitting in the Speaker's Chair and pressing all the buttons. Invariably, these functions were a great success, the setting was magnificent, all that was wanting was some public representatives who could raise their eyes above the small parochial quarrels, but unfortunately this proved to be beyond many of them.

Early in November I went and saw Harold Wilson at 10 Downing Street. Earlier, in October, I had been to see Frank Soskice at the Home Office. Frank, who became a friend like all Home Secretaries, was one of the nicest people I had ever met. My visit was, however, largely a courtesy call. The Prime Minister arrived late as he had not then moved into No 10 and he was on his way to catch the train to Liverpool.

I also went to the Department of Economic Affairs to see George Brown. He and his wife, Sophie, soon became, and have always remained, friends. I got him interested in the large Belfast freighter which was being built at Shorts. The RAF had only ordered ten of these. If George had had his way he would have got the order increased. Proud of his Irish ancestry, he felt he would like to do something for some part of Ireland, even though his forebears came from Cork. But as a devout Anglo Catholic he found Protestant Ulster a bit hard to stomach! So long as he remained at the DEA, and with his interest in regional development, he was one of our best friends. His policies were better suited to our needs than those of the Conservative Party.

In the middle of November a post-mortem on the first Ulster Week at Nottingham was held at Stormont Castle. The manufacturers themselves hailed it as a great success and with their enthusiasm to back us we announced that the next Week would be held in Bristol. This set in train a programme of two Ulster Weeks a year in many of the major cities of Britain. They were abruptly brought to an end by the Ulster Week in Birmingham in April 1969, at the moment when I was being 'blown' out of office by explosions, allegedly set off by extreme Protestants. These explosions not only achieved their main purpose, but put the prosperity and future of Ulster at stake.

December saw the arrival of a new Governor of Northern Ireland. Lord Erskine had for several years been Chairman of the Northern Ireland Joint Exchequer Board, which existed to smooth out any problems which might arise between the Treasury and the Ministry of Finance. Unlike his predecessors, he always took the trouble to come over for the Northern Ireland budget and while Minister of Finance I got to know him well. There was, however, another angle to his appointment. All the previous governors had been Anglicans, and although I was one myself, I thought it was high time that we had a Presbyterian. This denomination is the most numerous in Northern Ireland and it was unlikely that we would find a Presbyterian governor unless we went to Scotland. He was bold and adventurous as befits a businessman, which, of course, got him into trouble.

A Colonial Governor governs. A Governor of Northern Ireland is purely representational. After being used, as a businessman, to taking big decisions, he may have found the position irksome. In any case, he had to resign before his time owing to the indisposition of his charming wife, Netta. Today she and Jack are retired in their lovely

66

My father and mother

The first meeting between a Northern Ireland Prime Minister and a U S President in office.

In conversation with Willi Brandt.

In Atlanta, Georgia, with General Eisenhower and a copy of Magna Carta.

With Councillor Robert Hart, after opening O'Neill Road. The Paisleyites in the background are an example of what I had to contend with.

The first ever visit of a Northern Ireland Prime Minister to a Catholic school. It was a similar picture that was reproduced in Paisley's *Protestant Telegraph*.

The first ever visit of a Prime Minister of the Republic to Northern Ireland. Sean Lemass and myself walk into a battery of cameras after lunch at Stormont House.

In Dublin with Jack Lynch (then Minister for Industry and Commerce),
Frank Aiken (Minister for Foreign Affairs) and Sean Lemass.

With William Craig and Brian Faulkner after a working lunch with
Harold Wilson.

With my wife, Jean, and Cardinal Conway.

With Jack Lynch and Ken Whitaker at Stormont House.

With Eamon De Valera, President of the Republic of Ireland, in Phoenix Park, Dublin.

Georgian flat in Edinburgh and I thank them for all that they tried to achieve.

As 1964 drew to a close details of Professor Tom Wilson's economic plan began to emerge and the *Belfast News Letter* wrote a glowing leader on the subject entitled 'Face Lift to meet the New World'. The final sentence read, 'For him [myself] and for Ulster, history may yet record 1964 as a turning point, as a year of greatness.' The future of Ulster was wrecked, not by Treasury meanness, not by lack of forward looking, thinking and planning, but by outdated bigotry. We had all the benefits of belonging to a large economy, which were denied to the Republic of Ireland, but we threw it all away in trying to maintain an impossible position of Protestant ascendancy at any price.

8

 The North-South Meetings

As the Christmas recess of 1964 turned into the New Year of 1965 I began to ponder upon the future. In March I would have held the premiership for two years. By now, after twenty-one months in office, I felt sufficiently secure to take some bold initiative in order to try and break Northern Ireland out of the chains of fear which had bound her for forty-three years.

One evening early in January I summoned my advisers to the then official residence, Stormont House. I gave it as my considered view that I should ask Mr Lemass, the Prime Minister of the Republic, to lunch at Stormont House in a few days time. After a lengthy discussion it was finally agreed that, on balance, it was the right thing to do.

The story of how the meeting was arranged has often been told in Northern Ireland. Indeed immediately after the meeting I did about three programmes on television and sound in which I told and retold the story. But for those outside Northern Ireland, and indeed in order to paint a more detailed picture, I would now like to give a fuller version of these events as I remember them now, some six years later.

At the various World Bank meetings where I was usually accompanied by my Private Secretary, Jim Malley, I met and made friends with Ken Whitaker, then head of the Ministry for Finance in Dublin. Obviously as head of the Civil Service he would be the man to contact, and as Jim Malley knew him well he would be the man to make the contact. After all, we did not even know if Mr Lemass would accept the invitation.

At first Jim thought of going down to Dublin by car and of course from the point of view of security this would undoubtedly have been the best way to travel. It may surprise those who live outside Ireland that it is perfectly normal for people to drive all over Ireland in their own cars and the formalities at the border are of the most rudimentary kind—usually a wave at the man in the customs hut. He rang up Ken Whitaker and arranged to have lunch with him at the Shelbourne Hotel in Dublin, but as the day approached the weather got worse and with the threat of snow he decided to go by train.

On arrival at the station in Belfast the first person he met was his sister, up from Tyrone for a day's shopping. He swore her to secrecy about the fact that she had met him, as he felt this was the only thing he could do in all the circumstances. He then climbed into a carriage only to find that Arthur Algeo, head of the Northern Ireland Transport Authority, was already there. As they knew each other well he could only make the best of the situation. Within minutes a BBC cameraman came in to photograph Algeo who was going down to Dublin for the inauguration of a new bus service between Dublin and Belfast. Jim was able to hide behind his newspaper while the floodlights were turned on, because, of course, he knew and was known by all the cameramen in Belfast. Mercifully he was not detected, but a man with slower reflexes might already have given the show away! To Algeo, who was wondering why he was on the train, he said that he was visiting a cousin in Dublin and that the Christmas recess was the only occasion when he could find the time. Soon Algeo told him that when he got to Dublin he would be met by a car from CIE, the Southern Transport Authority, and that he would like to give him a lift. Jim thanked him and said that he was lunching with a Civil Service friend in the Ministry for Finance before he went on to his cousin. Sir Arthur Algeo is now dead, but Jim wondered at the time whether he didn't suspect something. Certainly if he did he kept it to himself, for which we must all be grateful.

During lunch Jim unfolded the situation to Ken Whitaker, who was undoubtedly surprised. Shortly before Malley left I had a last minute idea and told him that if possible he must see Mr Lemass himself. I was worried that messages passed through various hands might be transmogrified *en route*. So during lunch Jim made it plain that if possible he wanted to see the Prime Minister himself. On their return to Ken Whitaker's office they discovered that Mr Lemass was engaged in a television recording programme, so an interview was booked for about 4.30 p.m.

Lemass was surprised when Ken arrived with Jim and even more surprised when Jim 'popped the question'. He said he would like to think about it and consult his colleagues, but accepted the invitation in principle. It was agreed that a letter would be sent by Whitaker to

Malley stating whether the invitation was acceptable and if the suggested date, 14 January, was suitable.

We waited for about a week and then as the agony of suspense became too great, Jim rang up Ken. He was mortified. The letter had been sent off the day after their meeting and had been typed out by his own personal secretary. Moreover she had taken it out and posted it herself, so as to avoid it going through the official mail where idle chatter might have made the meeting impossible. However, we now knew by telephone that the show was on and made preparations accordingly. Another two days were to pass before the fateful letter arrived and then it was all too obvious why it had not arrived earlier. It was addressed to: Sqdn Ldr J. Y. Malley, DSO, DFC, Stormont Castle, *Dublin*. In pencil below someone had written 'Try Belfast'. It appears that the unfortunate lady was so nervous when typing out this envelope that in a moment of stress she had written the address of the city to which she was most accustomed. Today this envelope is one of Jim's most treasured possessions and will become a family heirloom!

The day before the visit I informed the Minister of Finance, who was the most senior minister in the Cabinet. The Governor of Northern Ireland, Lord Erskine, already knew and approved. That night there was a gale and as I lay in bed at Stormont House I wondered how everything would go the next day. The following morning we rang round the other ministers to tell them and also informed the Chairman of the Party. The ministers were all asked to come to Stormont House for tea.

The night before, however, we were nearly scuppered. Mr Lemass had consulted too many of his colleagues and some ten days had now elapsed since the consultations. Tongues must have been wagging in Dublin. The Secretary to the Northern Ireland Cabinet, Sir Cecil Bateman, was rung up by the press and asked whether it was true that Mr Lemass was coming to visit me. It was plain that the press didn't know the date. Bateman's reply was masterful. 'I am,' he said, 'with the Prime Minister every day. If there is anyone who would know whether there is any truth in this story, I am the man.' He then rang off. It so happened that Mr Lemass was due to speak at Queen's University, Belfast, in a few weeks time and the press felt that they had plenty of time in which to check the story as they thought that in all probability he would combine a visit to Queen's with one to me. Mercifully for the safety of our visitor, and the image of Ulster, they decided not to 'print and be damned'.

To be fair to Mr Lemass, apart from some of his ministers whom he consulted before he accepted the invitation, he told no one, not even his wife, as I was to discover on my return visit a short time later. My driver, Raymond Hueston, had taken a few days off and so I told my relief driver, Jack Thompson, to look after Mr Lemass's driver. I shall always remember the story he told me afterwards. Apparently Mr Lemass's driver was at home the night before when someone rang up and told him to fill the car full up with petrol as he would be going for a long drive the next day. The driver was surprised but not his wife. She told her husband that she felt sure he was going to Belfast to 'visit Captain O'Neill'. He dismissed this idea as idiotic. The next day he went to pick up Mr Lemass, who, when he got into his car, slammed the door and said, 'Belfast, please'. Ken Whitaker also went to elaborate ruses to mislead everybody, including his family, and make them think that he was going to the office for the day.

That morning, in addition to telling the whole Northern Ireland Cabinet, we informed the Home Office. I also thought that as I happened to know him well, I would ring up Sir Saville Garner, the head of the Commonwealth Relations Office. In the event, I only spoke to Joe Garner about half an hour before Mr Lemass arrived. He was dumbfounded and delighted.

At nine o'clock that morning a police car reported to Stormont Castle to collect 'Mr Malley'. The driver had no idea where he was going until Jim got into the car. The previous evening when I had seen the head of the police he had two reactions. First he was—to my surprise—delighted about the meeting, feeling that improved relations between North and South would lead to improved relations between the majority and the minority in Northern Ireland. Secondly, he thought it better not to tell the police who was coming in case the news would get out. In any case, the police car, equipped with radio, would act as a police escort to Lemass's car into which Jim Malley would climb at the border. One other matter remained to be attended to. The Ministry of Finance would ring the customs post on the border at 11 a.m. to warn them that Mr Lemass was arriving in half an hour and tell them that everything was all right and that he was not to be stopped other than for Malley to greet him and get into his car.

At 11.15 a.m. Jim arrived at the border, walked into the British customs hut and asked, 'Were you surprised at the telephone message?' To which he received the astonishing reply, 'What message, the storm has broken our phone?'! He had some difficulty in persuading

71

them that Mr Lemass really was coming and that it wasn't all a hoax, but when he actually arrived their doubts were put at rest.

It had been decided that the news would be released at 1 p.m., at the moment that he arrived at Stormont House. This would mean that the world would know as he stepped out of his car, but not before. History will show that this was a wise precaution. At 12.55 p.m. I received a message to say that he was five minutes away. As I stood in the hall the thought occurred to me that a wrong word would wreck the meeting before it had started. It could even be that the future of Northern Ireland and of Southern Ireland might depend on mutual cordiality. 'Welcome to Ulster' would rub salt into a wound. 'Welcome to Northern Ireland' would be better, but might be a little 'troublemaking'. Finally, just as the car was arriving I hit on the right idea.

I went out and opened the door of the car. 'Welcome to the North', I said. There was no reply. A very warm greeting from Ken Whitaker helped to mollify me.

I helped Mr Lemass off with his coat and suggested that after his long drive he would probably like to wash his hands. Eventually, in the rather spacious loo at Stormont House he suddenly said, 'I shall get into terrible trouble for this.' 'No, Mr Lemass,' I replied, 'it is I who will get into trouble for this.' I then took him into the drawing room and introduced him to my wife and Cecil Bateman and Ken Bloomfield of the Cabinet Office staff. From then on he thawed out and became a very pleasant and amusing guest.

After lunch we walked up to Stormont Castle, the Cabinet offices, about a hundred yards away, and as we neared the entrance we saw more pressmen and photographers than I had ever seen in my life.

During the afternoon in my office we discussed various ways in which we might co-operate for our mutual benefit. I remember at one point he suggested that we should try to attract industry as one unit. I explained to him that the greatest single weapon in the armoury of the Ministry of Commerce in Belfast was the denial of an Industrial Development Certificate by the Board of Trade in London. I further explained to him that we were a Development Area within the UK and that the generous assistance, grants, etc which we paid to industrialists willing to set up plants in Northern Ireland were available because of our membership of the UK. I also pointed out that the Treasury would never agree to a venture which might mean that their funds were directly or indirectly going to assist a country outside the Commonwealth. He immediately understood all this and realised that it was useless to pursue this line of argument any further.

I found that like so many Irishmen he had a wonderful command of the English language. On our way down to Stormont House for tea he suggested that I should postpone the return visit to Dublin until the weather was better, but I replied that I felt that unless I came right away I might find that pressure would be put on me to refuse to go. At Stormont House the Cabinet were waiting to meet him and over tea many of those who have since pretended that they never wanted to meet the Taoiseach appeared to be delighted to see him.

When you are blazing a trail, when you are taking an action which none of your predecessors have thought wise to take in forty-three years, you may make some mistakes, but looking back I have no doubt that by and large we handled a difficult situation with as much skill as we could muster at that time. A few weeks later the whole Unionist Party supported a motion in favour of the meeting with two exceptions. One was a member who had been forced out of the Party in my predecessor's day and was expelled by my successor. The other was Edmond Warnock, the ex-Attorney General who had given my predecessor so much trouble. By Northern Ireland standards this was a smashing victory. Had I discussed the possible meeting with MPs either within or without the Cabinet it would undoubtedly have leaked to the media of information, as it did in Dublin, and then what would have happened to our guest?

There was one immediate tangible result from my meeting with Mr Lemass. The leader of the Nationalist Party, Eddie McAteer, went down to Dublin to see Mr Lemass. As a result of that meeting the Nationalist Party, for the first time in Northern Ireland's history, decided to form themselves into an official opposition party, which obviously made for an improved working of Parliament. I was delighted at the time, though my thoughts were tinged with sorrow. Tom Boyd, the leader of the small Labour Party, was a man for whom I had a great affection and respect. He had played his difficult role with great dignity and I was sorry to see him lose his position— which had no monetary rewards but nevertheless gave him a position in the Northern Ireland community.

Though it is chronologically out of order, I think I must here continue with a second meeting, with Mr Jack Lynch. It is always easier to repeat something which you have already done, rather than to blaze a trail, and so some time after Mr Lemass's retirement I got the Cabinet to agree that a meeting would be arranged at some

73

propitious moment with Mr Jack Lynch. For the second meeting then it was only necessary to approve the date, the decision had already been taken. The press, of course, would have liked to have advance information as to 'when and where' so that they could cover the event. I was prudent enough not to fall into that trap. Once again it was to be winter and on this occasion the Cabinet came to lunch instead of tea. It was nearly two years since the previous meeting and as it was getting near Christmas—11 December—we had plum pudding. The lunch was cooked by our daughter, Anne, and there are photographs in existence to show that some of today's leading extremists appear to be in paroxisms of pleasure about the meeting!

To some extent we were influenced by the press criticism about undue secrecy over the first meeting, so with the approval of Mr Jack Lynch, whom I had met on the return visit to Dublin in February 1965, we decided to release the news of Mr Lynch's visit as he crossed the border into Northern Ireland. Someone or other decided to pass on the information to Mr Paisley, possibly in order to get some good pictures and sensational news, and as a result as Mr Lynch's car circled round Carson's statue at Stormont it was snowballed by Mr Paisley and some of his ministers who had just had time to assemble there.

After Christmas in January 1968 I once again paid a return visit to Dublin. Once again we announced the visit as I crossed the border and once again extremists were given time to act. As our post-prandial discussions were drawing to a close in Iveagh House a worried official came to say that we would have to return by a very circuitous route as if we went back by the main road, or indeed anywhere through County Down at all, we would be shot by the IRA. So we had to return via County Armagh and the following evening I was criticised by the Belfast evening paper for not having the courage to return by the main road. I had to suffer in silence even from a liberal paper like the *Belfast Telegraph* which normally supported my policies!

Here I think I should sum up the advantages and disadvantages of these two meetings and the way they were handled. More important perhaps than anything else, we should assess the effect that the first ever meeting between a Prime Minister of the Republic and a Prime Minister of Northern Ireland had on the people of Northern Ireland in general, and the Unionist Party in particular.

Much has been written to suggest that if only I had told many more people about Mr Lemass's proposed visit, fourteen days before it took place (a) they would have wholeheartedly welcomed it, and

(b) the country as a whole would have accepted it. I am afraid that even after six years I do not agree with such a suggestion. First of all it would have been impossible to get agreement. Secondly, the proposed meeting would have leaked out long before the event and so endangered the life of my distinguished guest. We already know that it had leaked out in Dublin owing to the fact that senior members of the Cabinet had been consulted several days before.

The real test of Northern Ireland opinion came in the autumn, only some nine months after the Lemass meeting, and when the event was fresh in everyone's memory. I called an election in October 1965 with polling day in November. Moreover our manifesto could have stood inspection in any country in the world; for the first time it had no sectarian overtones or undertones. I spent a lot of time during that election canvassing in Catholic and Protestant houses in Belfast where trouble has since erupted. In both I had a tremendous reception. No previous Prime Minister of Northern Ireland had canvassed in Catholic houses for Unionist votes, but despite publicity and pictures to that effect, my reception in the Protestant houses was equally warm. The unfortunate Labour Party which in my predecessor's day had been gaining strength in each election and which some sections of the press were forecasting would double its representation at that election, was in fact practically annihilated. Where was the backlash against my invitation to Mr Lemass? It did not exist except in the minds of the extremists who had hoped that they could use the occasion to install a more reactionary Cabinet, and whose hopes were unfulfilled. We swept the country to a degree which surprised everyone including myself. Co-operation between North and South was now publicly endorsed, and today when a militant Protestant housewife fries an egg she may well be doing it on Catholic power generated in the South and distributed in the North as a result of that first O'Neill-Lemass meeting.

With a few shining exceptions, the Protestant clergy were too frightened to give a welcome to the meeting in case they offended some of their flock. A notable exception was a Presbyterian clergyman in my own area who on the Sunday immediately following told his congregation that I had done the right thing. At that particular time clerical support might have been helpful and I remember how worried Jack Sayers, the editor of the *Belfast Telegraph*, was that it was not forthcoming. Today I fear few people pay very much attention when the clergy speak out, though of course we must not underestimate the influence of those who have displayed consistent courage over several years, small though their numbers may be.

If, then, the election at the end of 1965 proved that my policies were acceptable to the vast majority of Protestants and a growing number of Catholics, when and where did things start to go wrong? The short answer is in the following year, in 1966. Moreover the cause, though deeply Irish, had little or nothing to do with Northern Ireland itself.

9
1965 and 1966

I T was fortunate that I called the election in 1965, for 1966 turned out to be the most difficult period I had encountered. In Northern Ireland it is always wise to have a Stormont election at a different time from the national election for Westminster. Once the September-October period for a Westminster election had passed in 1965, there seemed to be a real danger that Harold Wilson, tired of governing with a majority of four, would go to the country in the spring of 1966. So in order to avoid a clash with London I decided to call the election in October. It took the Opposition by surprise because it had already been announced that I was going to America as the guest speaker for the annual meeting of the English Speaking Union in Atlanta, Georgia. Having made the announcement about polling day in November I flew off to fulfil this engagement. I have already described my fascinating talk with ex-president Eisenhower, who kindly took me to the opening ceremony in his car. A copy of Magna Carta had been brought out for the occasion, and after the opening ceremony of the English Speaking Union meeting, where Eisenhower had made suitable remarks about the similarity between the English and the American laws and customs, we were both photographed one on either side of this ancient English document. There was, however, one other extramural activity which I remember well. A visit to the Lockheed plant in Atlanta. Shorts, who later got an order for podding the Rolls-Royce engine, were having talks with the firm and our visit coincided with the presence of the Managing Director of Short Brothers and Harland—little did we realise then how much the name of Lockheed would impinge itself upon the people of Britain six years later.

Returning after four days we had our smashing election victory.

To the outside commentator it seemed that 1966 would be an easier year than 1965. Moderation had paid off and the extremists could see that old attitudes and statements were not necessary in order to win elections. But things are never as simple as they seem.

1966 was the fiftieth anniversary of the Battle of the Somme. The Ulster Division had behaved with outstanding bravery and it was intended not only that we should visit France for certain ceremonies there, but also that the Queen would visit Northern Ireland. A new bridge was being built in the centre of Belfast and although it was typically Irish to call a bridge after a river, the idea was that it should be called the Somme Bridge.

When the 1914 war broke out the Irish Home Rule Bill had just become law. In order to achieve national unity the whole thing was put into cold storage for the duration of hostilities. The Ulster Volunteer Force, raised specifically by Carson to fight the British if they should try to coerce Ulster into an all-Ireland Parliament, was immediately put at the disposal of the British Government. This highly trained and disciplined body became one of the best divisions in the British Army. As 'the Somme' was their finest hour one would have thought that the Protestant extremists would have been satisfied with this name for the new bridge. Moreover, it would be hard for the Catholics to object to this name in memory of a battle where thousands of French Catholics were slaughtered in a vain attempt to push the German Army back. But seizing their opportunity, like the Communists at a poorly attended trade-union meeting, the extremists on the Belfast Corporation decided to call the new bridge after Carson. This obviously would infuriate the Catholics and might even incite the IRA to blow it up. The events in Northern Ireland since August 1969 show that this was not an unreasonable fear. Moreover, it was hoped that the Queen would open the bridge and the Governor of Northern Ireland, with whom she would stay, was understandably worried that the Queen might be embarrassed by hostile demonstrations, or alternatively that the bridge would be damaged before she opened it.

In the event another meeting at the Belfast City Hall decided by a majority to call it the Queen Elizabeth II Bridge. But the whole business, during which Carson's son was dragged over to Northern Ireland by Paisley, was a bad lead in to the Westminster election.

With the approach of Easter it became obvious that the Catholics in Belfast would insist on celebrating the Dublin Rebellion of 1916. Considering that Belfast was not involved in that event fifty years previously one might have hoped that those so minded would have contented themselves with attending the ceremony in Dublin, less than a hundred miles away. But all the indications were that there was no prominent Catholic prepared to give a lead in the interests of peace. I decided to form a committee consisting of all former Ministers of Home Affairs under my chairmanship and between us we survived the celebrations.

It was a difficult period because it soon became apparent that they would not content themselves with a one-day celebration, but insisted on inventing reasons why the celebrations should continue for some three weeks. The Catholic streets in Belfast became and remained a forest of Irish Republican flags for the duration of the celebrations.

Prior to the start of this difficult period I accepted an invitation to speak at a joint Protestant-Catholic meeting in order to try and take the heat out of the situation. Once again I was faced with an ice-breaking job. My predecessor had never attempted anything of this nature and therefore it was condemned by the Protestant extremists. During my remarks about the necessity for living together, I included the following delicately worded phrase about the divisiveness of separate education:

A major cause of division arises from the *de facto* segregation of education along religious lines. This is a most delicate matter and one must respect the firm conviction from which it springs. Many people have questioned, however, whether the maintenance of two distinct educational systems side by side is not wasteful of human and financial resources and a major barrier to any attempts at communal assimilation.

Two 'liberal' Nationalist MPs, the brothers Paddy and Tommy Gormley, both attended the gathering which I addressed and later when the Cardinal with the support of the hierarchy condemned me for my remarks I was defended by Paddy. On 22 April a headline in the *Belfast Telegraph* read 'Nationalist MP defends PM's speech'. He went further and said he was 'surprised' at the Cardinal's statement. In England this would be a normal state of affairs but in Ireland for a Catholic and Nationalist MP to attack his Cardinal and defend a Protestant Prime Minister was certainly progress of some kind! I don't think either side realised that there was no need for me to push myself out on a limb just before the Republican celebrations began. As I drove through the screaming Protestant pickets on my way to this remote building, called Corymeela, on the cliffs above the Atlantic, near Ballycastle, I wondered whether this particular piece of 'bridge building' had been worthwhile, but as I look back I am sure it was. We got through these lengthy Easter celebrations unharmed. No policeman was killed trying to enforce an impossible ban and we could look forward to the 'Somme celebrations' in France and the Queen's visit in July.

Paisley, wisely from his point of view, decided to use the resentment in extreme Protestant circles against the Republican celebrations in order to stage a series of meetings and marches. They became more noisy and violent until he staged a demonstration outside the General Assembly of the Presbyterian Church. The Governor, Lord Erskine, a Scottish Presbyterian, attended the meeting. As a result of the scenes outside, Lady Erskine became quite ill. There was widespread resentment among moderate people at what was now appearing to be an increasing tendency towards demonstration and violence, but I don't think anyone then realised that the Protestant marches of 1966 would be copied by the Civil Rights marches of 1968. I am not suggesting for a moment that the Civil Rights movement would not have got under way in any case, and presumably the example of Martin Luther King was in the forefront of their minds when they started in October 1968. Nevertheless, when they saw the notoriety which Paisley achieved for himself in 1966, they must have realised that only in such a manner could they achieve fame and TV coverage in 1968. As so often happens in life, those who are most adamant are those who are most likely to fail and ruin their cause. Charles I by being adamant and unreasonable nearly brought the British monarchy to an end as well as losing his own head. Fortunately for the monarchy Cromwell was even more adamant and unreasonable. As a result of these seventeenth century events the British monarchy is one of the few to survive today. Even when so soon after the restoration James II became quite impossible the British people did not try another dictator, but rather did they turn to that great Ulster hero, William of Orange.

In just the same way, if Ulster does not survive, then historians may well show that it was the Protestant extremists, yearning for the days of the Protestant ascendancy, who lit the flame which blew us up. This, of course, was coupled with the fact that for far too long no effort had been made to make the minority feel that they were wanted or even appreciated.

As Jean and I were leaving for Paris towards the end of June, news was coming through that some apparently innocent Catholic youths had been gunned down as they emerged from a pub. Two were wounded and one, Peter Ward aged 18, was killed. We had been looking forward to our French visit. Our Ambassador, Patrick Reilly, had actually called to see us in Belfast before taking up his post in Paris and it was typical of him that he should invite us to stay at the Embassy on our way to the Somme ceremony.

We were just being shown our room upstairs when an anxious official told me I was wanted on the telephone. It was the Chief Whip, Major Chichester-Clark. After he had filled me in on the latest situation since the shooting in Malvern Street, it was agreed that I would have to return in order to make a statement in Parliament the following day. The elaborate programme arranged for the first official visit of a Prime Minister of Northern Ireland to Paris was chucked out of the window. Arrangements were made for me to fly back that afternoon. Ken Bloomfield and I just had time to attend a lunch given in our honour by the Minister for Ex-Service Affairs. It was the first and last time that I walked up a staircase lined by the *Garde Republicaine*. My wife had to stand in for me at the banquet at the Embassy the following night. All the guests had been specially invited because they had been, or might be, useful to Northern Ireland, but I never saw the guests or the table laid with Wellington's gold plate. However, I got back in time for the moving and memorable trip to the Somme. Field Marshal Alexander was one of the veterans who attended.

Two things stand out in my memory. One was the service at the Ulster Tower on a perfect summer's morning, where I read the lesson. And when the Southern Irish feel hostile to the Old Ulster Volunteers I hope they will realise that the latter were practically all killed and injured fighting in the same war and on the same side as the thousands of Irish Volunteers who flocked to the British colours of their own free will.

The other memory is of the previous evening when we attended a wonderful Canadian ceremony at Newfoundland Park, Beaumont Hamel. Here the Newfoundland memorial was lit for the first time and the Band of the Royal Canadian Air Force beat retreat. After the ceremony the memorial was to be lit in perpetuity.

During my thirty-six hours back in Belfast it became plain, from a midnight meeting of ministers, that the ghastly, unprovoked event, which might have been a triple murder if the other two injured youths had been killed, had probably been carried out by the so-called Ulster Volunteer Force. Using a revered name in Ulster they were in a position to get support from unthinking, militant Protestants. The following day in the House of Commons I named the Ulster Volunteer

Force as an unlawful association under the Special Powers Act. This was a traumatic experience for Ulster Protestants who had always regarded the Special Powers Act as something which was for use only against the IRA. However, it got a general welcome from the press and from all moderate people.

It is strange to read that back in France 'Captain O'Neill was given a standing ovation by the Ulster veterans. One old soldier, wearing the colours of the original Ulster Volunteer Force told him amidst loud applause: "You and the Government are to be congratulated for laying on this pilgrimage."' Obviously these old boys knew the difference between the real UVF and its new namesake.

In July the Queen and the Duke of Edinburgh paid their visit. Even though a brick was dropped on the bonnet of the Royal car from a new building in process of erection, the visit was a great success. But for the murder of the previous week the Queen would probably have mentioned how glad she was that community relations were improving. We can still, however, read between the lines of her farewell statement radioed from the Royal aircraft. 'I hope that with the growth of mutual respect and understanding between all people in the Province, Northern Ireland will enjoy a prosperous future.' I found the Duke of Edinburgh very understanding and anxious that community relations should improve. How tragic that the Queen's hopes should have been so shattered since August 1969.

The seeds of 1966, germinating in 1968, unfortunately have now bloomed into violence.

Towards the end of July Paisley's case with regard to his conduct outside the Presbyterian Assembly in June came before the courts. As he would not agree to sign a bail bond to be of good conduct, he went to prison. However, as he was given time to sign he was able to address a rally on 'Why I chose jail'. This at least made it plain to anyone who wanted to understand that he had himself chosen to go to jail. Few people, however, remember this today, for time has erased it from their memories.

Early in August I went to Downing Street for lunch. I was accompanied by the Permanent Secretary to the Cabinet and Roy Jenkins, who had succeeded Frank Soskice as Home Secretary, was also there. I had already struck up a friendship with Roy and the party was a friendly one. Harold Wilson had in the preceding fortnight been to Moscow and Washington and in July 1966 restrictive measures had been introduced. I was fully expecting our little lunch party to be postponed, but not so. As I walked into the room upstairs on the way to the little dining room I could hardly believe my eyes. There he was, relaxed and happy and unmoved by world events. 'Terence, you know,' he said to Roy, 'came to see me when I was Leader of the Opposition, he didn't wait till I got to Downing Street.' As usual the photographic memory was at work. He confessed that in his travels East and West he had taken one sleeping pill for the first, and he hoped, the last time. But even so, he was in staggeringly good shape.

After a relaxed lunch we moved into the room that has windows overlooking St James's Park and others towards Horseguards Parade. There, with all the normal post-prandial ingredients, we settled down to a talk. 'I suppose,' said the Prime Minister, 'Northern Ireland is rather like Rhodesia.' 'Maybe it is,' I replied, 'but I do not intend to be the Garfield Todd of Northern Ireland.' He took the point immediately and then moved on to his next question. 'Why are you pursuing a policy which is so unpopular with the Protestants when you could, for instance, have decided not to meet Mr Lemass?' I explained at length my reasons and both Ministers welcomed the fact that the meeting had taken place.

As we went downstairs and passed all the prints of former Prime Ministers I had an uncontrollable urge to ask him a question. 'Can you hang here,' I asked, 'while you are still in office?' 'No,' he replied, 'but you can hang at Chequers ... By the way,' he added, 'I'm not sure I like that question, I'm not going to hang here for a very long time!' As we walked through the front hall he called for his pipe when he saw the summer crowds through the windows. The shaking of hands as we emerged was a professional affair—very different from the friendly amateur efforts with Sir Alec Douglas-Home, but then Harold Wilson is a professional through and through. If physical vigour and enjoyment of office were sufficient to sustain him, then he was going to be at No 10 for a long time to come!

Harold Wilson and Roy Jenkins knew only too well what a difficult summer we had survived and merely intended to have a talk in general terms which could be repeated later as and when appropriate. There had been more extremist trouble in Belfast at the end of July, due in part to Paisley going to jail, and the Government had been forced to put a three months ban on processions in and around Belfast. However, despite the problems which September was going to bring, the *Belfast News Letter*, the strongly Unionist morning paper, was able to write in a leader preceding the Downing Street talks— 'The meeting is taking place at a time when the stature of the Ulster

Premier, both at home and abroad, has never been higher.'

Lady Carson, the second wife of Lord Carson, died as soon as I returned from London. She had always supported me when I was in any trouble and I knew she must have been very unhappy about the events of the spring. However, her son, Ned, indicated that he would be happy if I would come to the funeral. We both went to it in the tiny church near her home in Kent. As the service proceeded with all the normal (perhaps rather higher than normal) Anglican cere- monial I couldn't help thinking how shocked the Ulster Protestants would have been. Two huge candles flanked the coffin and as the service proceeded I thought of Paisley's application from prison to attend this ceremony. Presbyterians, let alone the Free Presbyterians, would have been, to say the least, surprised! Ruby Carson was one of the most charming people I have ever met.

Newry is a Catholic town near the border and on the main road from Belfast to Dublin. Frank Cousins was attending a Trades Union Conference there. Norman Kennedy, who was the local Sec- retary of the Transport and General Workers' Union, asked me to come and open it. It was through Norman, later to become Northern Ireland's Senator Kennedy, that the arrangements for recognising the Trades Unions were effected. Frank Cousins mentioned this in his speech and we were all basking in reflected glory and admiration! I also had a very warm welcome from the Newry Council at the Town Hall. Before I could get away from the Civic reception nearly everyone in the room requested an autograph and I stayed much longer than originally intended. Both occasions bring back happy memories as I write these words nearly five years later.

September saw Jean and I setting out for the Ulster Societies' Annual Meeting in Manchester, and after ten days holiday in England we were due to go to Newcastle upon Tyne for one of our Ulster Trade Weeks. While in Norfolk news began to filter through about a back-bench conspiracy. It was alleged that a member called Boal, who represents the Shankill Road, was collecting signatures of those who wanted me to resign. As a piece of paper had received ten signatures in my predecessor's day, and only shortly before he resigned, I felt that this was possibly true and moreover that probably the same people would sign it. My first reaction was to return home, but I was advised that the best method of dealing with the situation was to play it cool. In Lincolnshire, our next port of call, there were more messages of more signatures, and this continued while we spent two nights at the Mansion House in Newcastle upon Tyne as the guests of the Lord Mayor, for the Ulster Week.

On our return from England I was given a list of those who were supposed to have signed this mysterious piece of paper. The trouble was that officially no one knew anything about it. The next morning when a Cabinet meeting was over, I threw down the gauntlet and told my colleagues I was going to fight this conspiracy. It was interesting to watch the faces of my colleagues: most were glad that I had spoken out, but some were surprised—perhaps even dismayed.

Mercifully there was not long to wait, for a back-bencher soon informed the press that he had been asked to sign the 'piece of paper' and had refused. As soon as the news broke, the Chief Whip, Major Chichester-Clark, issued a statement supporting me. At the same time I recorded a statement on television, standing in the hall at Stormont Castle, in which I made it plain that though the conspirators pretended that they wanted a new Prime Minister what they really wanted were different policies. From this moment on the conspiracy began to crumble and Mr Faulkner, who had postponed a trip to America, decided to leave.

Later at a meeting of the Parliamentary Party stories emerged of a meeting at Brian Faulkner's house (he was then Minister of Commerce) at which Harry West (Minister of Agriculture) had been present. What, however, sticks out in my mind was my predecessor's contribution, which went approximately as follows: 'Once a General loses the support of his troops he should go. In this case I would suggest he should have six weeks in which to repair the damage by touring Unionist Associations and explaining that he really is a true blue Unionist of the old type. If at the end of the six weeks the Party is not satisfied, he should resign.'

In rather different circumstances, before World War I, Carson described a statement by Asquith's administration involving delay over an intended action as 'sentence of death with stay of execution'. Brookeborough also knew perfectly well that during that six weeks Paisley would emerge from jail and that there could well be further disturbances during the autumn. The man who had taken so few courageous steps during twenty years of so-called power was quite willing to lay the head of his successor on a delayed-action guillotine.

One Belfast MP, who had undoubtedly signed the 'piece of paper', issued a statement saying he had withdrawn from his previous position. One sentence in that statement was most revealing. 'He regretted that because of the indirect pressures of extremism, democratic decision within the Party was made more difficult.'

There was a tailpiece to 'the conspiracy'. When Brian Faulkner returned from America I had a little chat with him. I explained that I had no intention of staying on for a long time and that if, for instance, I retired when I was sixty, he would then be 53, the exact age of my predecessor when he had become Prime Minister. But I said that, in fact, I expected I would go long before that. I had actually already decided to retire in September 1969. By that time the Parliament would be nearly four years old and it would give my successor over six months to play himself in before he need have an election. Moreover I would then be 55—an appropriate age to start a new life. For six months after this chat co-operation was wonderful and when it ceased I didn't really blame Brian. I knew that the dominant power in the family was his father who was desperately anxious to see his son as Prime Minister while he was still alive.

A few days later we had an unexpected visitor in the person of Lady Gibbs, the wife of Humphrey Gibbs, the Governor of Rhodesia. Her son, Nigel, had come to Northern Ireland to do an attachment with Gallaghers, the tobacco company. Jean had been to visit Nigel in hospital. Only a few days after his arrival he had complained of feeling tired. After an investigation it was discovered that he would require some four months treatment before he would be fit again.

His mother, Molly Gibbs, one of the most charming people I have met, came and spent the night. At this time UDI appeared imminent, but had still not been declared. During dinner I casually remarked that if only it were possible for the Queen Mother to visit them it might do a lot to kindle loyalty to the Crown and interfere with the onward march of UDI. I made this suggestion knowing what a roaring success her previous visit to Salisbury had been. The following day, much to my surprise, Molly Gibbs said that while she could not speak for anyone, she believed my casual remark might contain the answer to a growing problem. There and then I decided to act. I had struck up a good working relationship with Harold Wilson and so I wrote to him. A member of my staff was going to London and he took the letter with him. As bad luck would have it, the Prime Minister had already left for his Party's Conference on the South Coast and so the manuscript letter was given to a secretary at Downing Street who promised to see that it was delivered.

About a week later I had a long letter assuring me that my suggestion had received the most careful consideration but had finally been rejected. I still sometimes wonder whether the Queen Mother, with her fantastic charm, could not have stopped the declaration of UDI.

Nigel Gibbs, now getting better, came to stay with us for Christmas. After he left I had another shot. Two things had happened in the interval. UDI had been declared and the Queen Mother had had an operation. Remembering that King George VI had been invited to recuperate in South Africa after a Nationalist Government had come to power, it occurred to me that the Queen Mother might be invited out to recuperate in Rhodesia, and her mere presence might make future negotiations easier. This last attempt was, I suppose, never a starter, but I felt that at least I had made a small effort to assist in an intractable problem. I had often wondered whether, if Sir Alec Douglas-Home had won the 1964 election, UDI would ever have been declared. Now I wonder whether a Royal visit could have helped, but I fear we shall never know. An uncle and godfather of mine, Johnny Parsons, often said to me that the two saddest words in the English language were 'too late'. They certainly refer to the white population in Rhodesia and may well also refer to the Protestants in Ulster. In this connection it is strange to remember that my friends in the Unionist Party used to say, 'the trouble is that you are going too far and too fast'. Little did they realise that in fact we were doing too little and too late. Moreover, a most revealing expression was used when reforms were discussed. 'Haven't we', they would say, 'given them enough concessions?' This, indeed, was the language of the master race.

And so 1966 drew to a close as I went to hospital to have a small hernia operation. While there, Eddie McAteer, the Leader of the Nationalist Party, came to visit me. Neither of us realised at that time that the co-operation which had started with the visit of Sean Lemass in 1965 had, in fact, been shattered by the insistence of the Belfast Catholics in celebrating the fiftieth anniversary of the Dublin Rebellion. It was 1966 which made 1968 inevitable and was bound to put the whole future of Northern Ireland in the melting pot. But unfortunately if you are an extremist you live for the present, while sacrificing the future. The execution of the leaders of the Rebellion in 1916 made it inevitable that the South would leave first the United Kingdom, and then the Commonwealth. The unreasonable attitude of extreme Unionists from the Paisley marches in 1966 to MPs un-willingness to have a Code of Conduct for ministers, made it inevitable that the whole future of Stormont would be put at risk. But reaction-ary attitudes and survival, as the Bourbons discovered, do not go hand in hand.

10

1967

NINETEEN hundred and sixty-seven was a year of travel in the sense that instead of just going to America, as we did nearly every year, we also paid an official visit to Germany. But I started the year with a trip to Downing Street. On my previous visit I had gone alone to No 10 and some people thought that a 'liberal' Prime Minister of Northern Ireland, alone with a Labour Prime Minister of the UK, must bode some evil tidings for Ulster. This time I decided to take Faulkner and Craig with me. This visit was largely a public relations exercise from Westminster's point of view, and Harold Wilson was out to show how tough he could be. Perhaps he rather over-played his hand!

After lunch, at which the conversation was general, we went down to the Cabinet Room. Pushing a box of cigars in Faulkner's direction, he asked him to take one. A look of horror spread over Brian's face. 'Have you got no vices?' the Prime Minister enquired. 'I see you drank nothing at lunch.' 'I'm not against smoking and drinking,' Brian replied. 'It is just that my father gave me £100 not to drink till I was 21.' 'Oh, I see,' said Wilson, 'you're earning the next £100 now.' It was some time before Brian regained his composure.

There was a rather pleasant incident which took place before we left for Germany. Ballymena, the Aberdeen of Northern Ireland, decided to follow popular trends and 'twin' with a town in the West of Ireland called Castlebar. Members of the Castlebar Chamber of Commerce came North and were given a wonderful time. I received them at Stormont and they presented me with a piece of their pottery with the arms of Ballymena and Castlebar surrounded by the names of these towns and the date—1967. 'TREMENDOUS RECEPTION FOR CASTLEBAR MEN IN NORTH' said the *Mayo News* on 4 February 1967. Later we were invited to attend the Annual Dinner of the Castlebar Chamber of Commerce in February 1971. Fortunately in my letter of acceptance I put in a caveat that if things were difficult in the North I might not be able to come. The invitation came from John MacHale who had been on the trip to Northern Ireland in 1967. A successful visit to Dublin in January 1971 to speak to the Publicity Club seemed to hold out hope for Castlebar, but it was not to be. Serious rioting in the North broke out soon after my Dublin visit, and in the middle of the postal strike I had to pass a message to Castlebar through our police. When the news broke in the papers it appeared that Castlebar had been plastered with anti-O'Neill slogans, presumably by the IRA, and everyone assumed that this was why I had put it off. For those in Britain who think that Irish problems are easy, there is perhaps a lesson to be drawn from this small episode. Nearly two years after I had resigned the premiership and doubtless partly because I had been given two standing ovations in Dublin, the extremists in the Castlebar area wanted to protest about North-South co-operation, even on a private basis. In such ways, for instance in the snowballing of Mr Lynch's car when he came to Stormont, is co-operation made difficult.

Towards the end of March we set off on our visit to Germany. Arranged by Herr Blankenhorn, the German Ambassador who had recently come to Northern Ireland, it was a pleasant occasion. On the first evening in Bonn there was a dinner party at the British Embassy given by our Ambassador, Sir Frank Roberts. Lady Roberts, of Lebanese extraction, had known my brother Brian before the war when the Irish Guards were stationed in Egypt. At that time Sir Frank had been secretary to our Ambassador in Cairo. On our return to our hotel my staff persuaded me to have a nightcap with them before I went to bed. We had hardly settled down before Mr Erskine Childers, a Southern Irish Minister, and his staff emerged from a late dinner in the hotel dining room. It was a very pleasant evening as it always is when Irishmen meet off their own soil!

Towards midnight I decided that the day which had started with a flight from London was far enough advanced and so I went up to bed and to tell Jean that Erskine Childers was in the hotel, the Kaiserhof on the Rhine. Hardly had I arrived upstairs than the telephone rang and Tommy Roberts, our excellent chief public relations officer in London, told me that Vice-President Humphrey would like to meet me in the morning. I began to wonder just who was *not* staying in the Kaiserhof. In the morning we went for a spirited walk down the Rhine surrounded by secret servicemen with walkie-talkies and cameramen taking endless photographs. It was a stimulating occasion. A motorcade followed us and finally, persuaded by his staff that he was very late for a policy conference of US Ambassadors at the American Embassy, we both climbed into a black Cadillac to complete the journey. I enjoyed meeting this friendly man enormously and I remember we discussed Edward Heath and I expressed the belief that if he could win the next election he might be a better Prime Minister than one would be led to believe by his performance as Leader of the Opposition. As I drove back to the hotel to collect Jean I remember thinking that perhaps Humphrey, nice though he was, would not make a good President. It is really rather arrogant the way one comes to quick conclusions of this kind, and this indeed is what journalists have to do. But just for the record, those were my impressions.

Our programme was now horribly behind-hand. We were paying an official visit to Duisburg and as we sped down the *autobahn* I was astonished to see German police standing to attention and saluting as we went under bridges. It was pouring with rain and we were over an hour late. One wondered where else in the world such courtesies would be paid in such conditions.

The Mayor of Duisburg gave a lunch for us and I see that I spoke, appropriately enough, about Gustav Wolff from Hamburg having started a shipyard in Belfast with the Englishman, Harland. I also mentioned the German firms which had factories in Ulster. There followed a visit to the enormous Thyssen steel works.

The following day started with a visit to Herr Willi Brandt, then Foreign Minister, at his official home on the outskirts of Bonn. I remember that we were given glasses of Sandeman's sherry at 10 a.m. This was most appropriate as my aunt Sylvia, Con O'Neill's mother, was a Sandeman before she married my uncle, Hugh Rathcavan (O'Neill). Moreover, I remember quite plainly early on in the talk Herr Brandt asked me, 'Is Sir Con your cousin?' and when I replied that he was, he added: 'We would very much like to see him as your next Ambassador here.' In view of subsequent events I would just like to put this on the record. But also for the record, George Brown is an old friend of mine, so I am not raising this point in any spirit of hostility.

I remember also explaining to him that there were many people in Britain hostile to our joining EEC, though the official Whitehall policy seemed to assume that we would inevitably one day be a member of the Community. He also explained to me that he was unable, at that point in time, to take a new initiative in putting pressure on General de Gaulle to be more reasonable. He was really expressing the hope that London understood that one could not go on throwing oneself against a brick wall on behalf of British entry. On my next visit to London I passed this view on to my cousin.

As Foreign Secretary in a coalition Government and leader of the minority Social Democratic Party in that Government, he was obviously in a difficult position. This former famous Mayor of Berlin somehow seemed to convey in conversation the strain under which he must have been operating. The meeting was most friendly and although I have never before drunk sherry at 10 a.m. in the morning, the occasion itself was extremely cordial!

This was our last day in Bonn and we drove on to Brunswick where we were the guests at lunch of the Government of Lower Saxony. It was interesting to see prints of George III and George IV in the building where we lunched. It was a reminder that they were also Kings of Hanover. Later that day we arrived at Wolfenbüttel where our son, Patrick, was stationed in the Queen's Royal Irish Hussars. This regiment, an amalgamation of the Fourth and the Eighth Hussars, has done a lot of recruiting in Northern Ireland and I had various duties to perform. With a bowler hat, a stiff collar and a Guards tie, the Commanding Officer was kind enough to say that I looked as military as I could in civilian clothes! It was a short weekend, but an interesting one. The armoured cars and their crews which we inspected were not all that different from the Second Battalion Irish Guards and their tanks twenty-five years before; while visiting places like the Sergeants' Mess seemed all too familiar. Having, however, only been a wartime soldier, I was staggered by the magnificence of the regimental plate.

On Sunday we went to church where Patrick played the organ, continuing a family tradition which goes back many generations.

In Berlin we stayed with John Nelson who was our Commander-in-Chief. Like other visitors, we were amazed at how much countryside there was within the confines of West Berlin. While there, the General's ADC took us into East Berlin in a military car. While the ADC in uniform did not require a passport, we showed ours through the windows, which were kept tightly shut. This process was necessary as guards had been known to snatch passports and then create an incident in delaying their return. It seemed strange that we could visit the famous Pergamon museum in company with a party of French sailors, but that the unfortunate West Germans were not allowed to see it. Interesting though it was, one was glad to get back to West Berlin again!

Pleasant visits to Munich and Stuttgart completed our German trip. Never before had a Prime Minister of Northern Ireland paid an official visit to Germany and for that reason, if for no other, it was breaking new ground. But above all, the publicity given by the German press would not be likely to come amiss while we were trying our best to attract industry to Northern Ireland.

Various suggestions were made that it should be followed by an official visit to France. Curiously enough, we have a French Consul in Belfast, the only other foreign representative being the American Consul General, and he was keen that we should go, but first the relationship between London and Paris was not favourable and later, once the Civil Rights movement got under way in the autumn of 1968, it obviously became impossible. While I was able to deliver prepared speeches in German, I would have been much more at home in French and was sorry that the opportunity did not present itself. However, we have two large factories from Michelin to remind us of the capacity of French industry.

When Brian Faulkner became Prime Minister he appointed Harry West as Minister of Agriculture. It is odd, therefore, to see a press cutting 27 April 1967 which reads, 'Mr West sacked by the Prime Minister'. This case emerged from my introduction of a Code of Conduct for Ministers during my first months of office. While I have not consulted Cabinet papers I have no keen recollection of either Faulkner or West pressing me to introduce such a Code, one of the many English features not adopted in Northern Ireland. I will content myself by saying that I was advised throughout by the Attorney General of the day and that those who are interested can always consult the Northern Ireland Hansard of that time. Harry West, though never a reformer, and whose most usual utterance was, 'Fermanagh will never stand for it', was nevertheless an entertaining member of the Cabinet and a good mixer. He once went to Russia on an agricultural visitation and the stories he told on his return kept us in fits of laughter. So long as Ulster was cosy and unreformed, Harry was well suited to office. I never remember having any unpleasant disagreement with him as he was the sort of person who it was hard to quarrel with. This made his dismissal all the harder. It would have been much easier if I had disliked him. But I was equally convinced that having drawn up a Code of Principles we had to stick to them.

One final point remains to be made about the West affair. Although there was no question of dishonourable conduct the Attorney General would undoubtedly have resigned if I had done nothing after all his painstaking labour in the affair. Nor was I prepared to introduce measures to keep up to British ministerial standards of conduct and then have them flouted. I fully realised that by sacking a popular minister I might be bringing about my own downfall, but I was determined to do what I believed to be right rather than to do what I knew to be popular. The proof of the pudding was in the eating. After the Attorney General had spoken in the House no one resigned from the Cabinet and the matter soon faded from public interest. It was just another occasion where pulling the country, kicking and screaming, into the twentieth century was difficult and painful.

In the autumn we undertook a hectic tour of America and Canada. Princess Alexandra was to open a British Week in Chicago, Dallas and Toronto. We followed on and met up with her at all these places. Our itinerary was as follows: New York, Philadelphia, Chicago, Seattle, San Francisco, Phoenix, Houston, Dallas, Washington, Toronto, Montreal, New York. All completed between 3 and 21 October. It was gruelling and never to be repeated. We often spent the weekend travelling and when we compared notes with the Royal travellers in Toronto we found that they had been wiser and rested at weekends. I was on television in every centre and from long experience I can truthfully say that I enjoy TV in America more than I do at home. The informality is what is so appealing. I have now done the 'Today Show' in New York three times and apart from having to get up at the crack of dawn, it is really great fun being interviewed by Frank Magee and Barbara Walters. Somehow the fact that you are being watched by about forty-five million people is an added stimulus. Curiously enough, the best television I have ever done anywhere was years ago in St Louis when I was Minister of Finance. I arrived five minutes late for a kind of Panorama show and the four professors who were there to interview me had to talk to each other till I arrived. The producer was thrilled with the result!

Looking back on this particular tour I would say the highlights were Chicago, where I was received by the Irish Mayor, Richard Daley,* and addressed the Executive Club, San Francisco, where I was received by another Irish Mayor, Shelley—both said their fathers would turn in their graves if they could see them receiving the Prime Minister of Northern Ireland! Dallas, where the wonderful Stanley Marcus kindly put on a Northern Ireland Day in the middle of the

* This was before Mayor Daley was ever heard of by the people of Britain.

British Week in his famous Nieman Marcus store, and Toronto, where Eatons, the largest chain of department stores in the world, kindly put a representation of the square in the village of Portglenone, County Antrim, where Timothy Eaton first worked in a shop. We were mobbed when we got to the top of this store by all the people of Ulster descent. Our tour ended with Expo' in Montreal, where we were the guests of Mr Chevrier, the minister in charge of the exhibition, who had just previously been Canadian High Commissioner in London.

It may have been exhausting, but it was nevertheless a memorable tour. Next year we were to have our last one and taking a leaf from the Royal travellers, we insisted on having our weekends free.

Immediately upon our return from America we visited the Guildhall where we were running an Ulster fashion show, which was to be attended by Princess Margaret. It was a great success. As so often on these occasions, things ran late and by the time we were free to leave we were very late. Our destination was Southampton where we were opening yet another Ulster Week.

We had so often taken part in one of those terrifying motorcades in North American cities, where police mounted on motorcycles rush one through red lights, sirens screaming, while one wonders whether one will ever reach one's destination alive. This time, for the first and last time, the City of London police put on a similar show which took us as far out as Guildford. It was the height of the rush hour and the whole performance was superbly executed. It was an Anglicised version of the American VIP treatment. Our Government driver, however, was as thankful as we were when things returned to normal in the Guildford area.

The Southampton effort was the smallest Ulster week we had ever put on. We were advised that we would attract people from Portsmouth and Bournemouth. I doubt, however, whether this worked out in practice. At least we had now covered the South coast in our selection of cities which had taken us from Edinburgh to Bristol in our series of Trade Weeks.

Nothing of great note took place at home, but November saw us back in London again. The new Lord Mayor, Sir Gilbert Inglefield, had kindly asked us to the Lord Mayor's Banquet and also to the Lord Mayor's Show, the previous Saturday. Jean could not manage the Show owing to a previous engagement, so I took Patrick instead. Sunday was Remembrance Day and Roy Jenkins kindly asked me to watch the Cenotaph ceremony from the Home Office. Afterwards we were all invited in for a drink. I soon saw Ted Heath deep in conversation with Neil Cairncross who looked after Northern Ireland's affairs in the Home Office, so I joined them. It was not long, however, before I saw the Prime Minister and Mrs Wilson smiling at the company I was in. I soon repaired the situation by heading his way. I had seldom seen him in better form. After a chat he said he would like to come to Northern Ireland, so I suggested he should bring Mary with him.

Monday 13 November was the day of the Lord Mayor's Banquet and Jean flew over for it. After the preliminary formalities were over some of us assembled in a small room. I saw the Prime Minister, but could tell that the cheerful mood he had displayed on the previous day had evaporated. Indeed, something told me that I had better keep away.

The feast soon began and someone seated next to me had not turned up. I could see that if George Brown did arrive I would, in fact, find myself next to him. He had been kept late at the office but he soon arrived. The Prime Minister, who spoke about European technological co-operation, made the worst speech I had ever heard him make. Nor did George Brown's muttered comments make it easier to listen to. By the end of the evening I was convinced that devaluation was upon us. I have only recently had confirmation of the march of events from Harold Wilson's memoirs. For we read that he had come straight from No 10 where he had just seen the Governor of the Bank of England, who was now leaning towards devaluation rather than acceptance of any package of aid accompanied by restrictions.

Returning from London I told my staff that I felt sure devaluation was on the way. We had, however, to wait till the end of the week to receive confirmation of my suspicions. On Friday a message came through from the Home Office to say that a special message from the Home Office would be flown over on Saturday which was to be given to me at 9 p.m. A member of the Cabinet Office staff was returning from London on Saturday, so he, in fact, brought it with him and gave it to my Permanent Secretary. We were attending a show that night which was being put on by the Arts Council. In the interval while refreshments were being consumed this impressive document was handed to me. Covered with heavy seals and with another envelope inside I eventually reached the enclosed letter. I retreated into a corner of the room to read it, and not being sure at what moment the news would burst upon the world, I decided to say nothing to anybody. At the time I wondered what the local dignitaries of the Arts Council imagined was contained in this impressive envelope. I stuffed it into the inside pocket of my dinner jacket and rejoined the assembled throng. If it were not the 'pound in my pocket' it neverthe-less contained information about the pound!

I have already dealt with the visit which Mr Lynch paid to Belfast in December and our return visit to Dublin in January. So 1967 came to an end, it had not been an eventful year. But 1968 was to usher in a new era. The repercussions from the first Civil Rights march are still with us as I write these words and are likely to remain with us for a long time to come. We will, however, let the events speak for themselves.

II

 1968

T HE Spring of 1968 passed without any great event. My predecessor, who had meant to retire from Parliament on his
resignation, was now able to do so five years later as he thought
it now possible that his son would be selected for his seat. Selection in
Ulster was always the important hurdle, and soon his son, who was
even more reactionary than the father, took his seat as Stormont. This
coincided with my fifth anniversary as Prime Minister.

My immediate staff kindly celebrated the occasion by giving me a
small and excellent dinner. The evening ended with a toast to the next
five years. I knew myself that this would be both impossible and
undesirable, but I could not tell anyone that the date I had in mind for
resignation was the autumn of 1969.

Various papers produced articles covering the quinquenium, among
them a Dublin paper, the *Irish Press*. In a large spread headed by an
imposing picture of Parliament Buildings, Stormont, I read in the
second paragraph: 'His efforts to establish greater harmony among
Catholics and Protestants in the North have not been as rapid as
many people up here would wish but the fact that he has succeeded
at all is a credit to a man who has had to ride some bitter storms both
inside and outside the Unionist Party.' It was nice to know that some
people South of the border, as well as those with more liberal sentiments in the North, appreciated one's efforts. The final paragraph,
however, reads somewhat strangely today. It suggests that North-
South meetings between the Prime Ministers of the two states will
become an accepted part of Irish political life.

Though nothing of any great note happened during the summer of
1968, there is one incident I should mention as it shows the kind of
prejudice I was up against in my efforts to improve community
relations.

I had been asked to go and address the Woodvale Unionist Association, and while the citizens in that area held extreme views, I had been told that the leadership of the Association itself was moderate, as indeed it turned out to be. Expecting that there might be pickets, I switched on the police radio in the car just in time to hear an officer explaining that owing to a football match in another part of the city, no more police were available for the meeting. Fortunately I took the demonstrators by surprise as I arrived from an unexpected direction. This and the magnificent efforts of the handful of police got me into the meeting unscathed. The people inside the meeting gave me a particularly warm and friendly reception. When it was over and I was enjoying the cup of tea which always follows meetings in Ulster, a senior police officer came and told me that the crowd had now grown to five hundred in the narrow street outside. My own car had been taken away in case it was overturned and a police car now awaited me. Moreover, the police thought that, on balance, it would be better if I left while it was still daylight.

Thoughts of a dignified departure were to vanish as the police propelled me into their car through a hail of missiles. The only direct hit I received was a pebble or a penny in the eye. By the time I got home it was quite badly inflamed, but Jean, with her wartime nursing experience, produced some ice and soon after its application it miraculously subsided.

It might all have been much worse. First, my relief driver, Jack Thompson, was as cool as a cucumber when we arrived, and the small number of policemen on duty had been quite magnificent. Otherwise it would have been impossible for the *Belfast Telegraph* to report the next day, 'Captain O'Neill stepped out smiling'. Secondly, the police were quite correct to remove the official car soon after I entered the Hall, otherwise it would at least have been overturned and probably burnt.

During the following twenty-four hours I learnt a lot more about the build-up to the trouble. Paisley had addressed the crowd just before I arrived on 'its right to protest', and a picture of me visiting a convent the previous weekend, in connection with the Civic Weeks we used to run, was publicly burnt.

People who have never been involved in such incidents find it hard to appreciate the problems with which one is faced. If one dashes too fast through a hostile crowd then someone will be injured or killed. If one goes too slowly, either a window will be broken, the car over-turned, or the tyres slashed. The essentials for success are a cool driver and efficient police pushing the people away from the car. In this particular case we managed to keep going at about eight miles an hour solely owing to the efficiency of the small handful of police.

For some years we had been in the habit of taking the car to Britain for a holiday in August. Our second stop was with Jean's cousin, Jack Harrington, in Herefordshire. One morning the telephone rang and it was Harold Black, the Permanent Secretary to the Northern Ireland Cabinet. Before leaving I had known that there was to be a march to Dungannon, but Northern Ireland being a country of marches, one tended to accept these things as normal. 'You might like to know,' he said, 'that the march to Dungannon passed off peacefully, though there were some anxious moments.'

I had already read *The Times* from cover to cover; there was not a word about it. Admittedly Russia had invaded Czechoslavakia and therefore there was much to fill the paper's pages, but even so one might have expected a paragraph somewhere. Had we all known it, that unreported Civil Rights march was to be the start of something which would shake Northern Ireland to its foundations, split the ruling Unionist Party, and initiate more reforms in two years than I had thought possible in ten. Moreover, Westminster, our sovereign Parliament, had Northern Ireland thrust on its plate as never before since the Government of Ireland Act of 1920.

However, no one at that date could fully have foreseen the passage of events. We ourselves were looking forward to what was to be our last visit to America and Canada, and this time, Newfoundland.

Apart from my usual visits to the large banks in New York, who were so helpful in inviting industrialists to meet and hear me at their luncheons, we were also billed to open the 'Great Festival of Great Britain' in Macy's new Colonie Store in the capital of New York State. This was a fabulous function, but first we called on Governor Rockefeller, who proudly threw up his office window so that we could see all the rebuilding going on in Albany.

Macy's was selling British goods in all its various New York stores, and no one who has not seen an American store promotion can have any idea what it is like. In my opening remarks I see that I said, 'Napoleon once referred to us as a nation of shopkeepers. For us in Britain there can be no two ways about it—we must trade to live'— and more in that vein. Then I was handed an immense pair of scissors with which I cut a vast ribbon. Someone had found out that it was my birthday and I was then presented with a five tier cake some four feet high. From long experience, the Board of Trade knew just how to help with these promotions. Colourful uniforms, British bobbies, bagpipes and London buses, are among the many complements to these events which I have seen at British promotions from Nieman Marcus in Dallas, Texas, to Toronto in Canada. Northern Ireland was able to add one trumpeter, a survivor of the 'Hillsborough Guard', which had originally been a kind of private army belonging to the Downshire family. He is now used for ceremonial occasions by the Governor of Northern Ireland.

The trip also included a visit to Pittsburgh, where we were magnificently looked after by the Mellon family. Earlier that year we had a wonderful gathering for the opening ceremony of the original Mellon homestead in County Tyrone. Fifty members of the Mellon family came to Northern Ireland headed by General Richard King Mellon. The whole project had been the brainchild of Doctor Matthew Mellon, and the Government of Northern Ireland had given all possible help. With a generous gift from the Mellon family this thatched farmhouse, now cared for by the National Trust, is open to the public. In Pittsburgh I was able to address leading industrialists as I had so frequently done before, and then there was a memorable weekend with the Mellon family at Ligonier.

We sat down twenty-four people for dinner on a Friday night in General Mellon's 'British country house' type home. We all had to wear medals and but for the accents it might have been a dinner in England before the war. The countryside was quite beautiful and the park-like surroundings added to the general illusion of being at home. The following day we had a wonderful visit to their shooting lodge, which was, in fact, the original home of the original Judge Mellon who had emigrated with his family at the age of five in 1813.

Even now, however, we hadn't quite learnt our lesson about having a full weekend away from travel and functions. Most of Sunday was spent flying to Montreal in a Shorts' Skyvan in order to give this aeroplane some publicity in Canada. Jean's finest hour was on the Saturday morning when General Mellon showed her his collection of coins. On enquiry she discovered that he hadn't got a Churchill crown, so dipping into her bag she tipped him five shillings!

In Montreal we were looked after by Jasper Cross, our Chief Trade Commissioner who I had first met in Winnipeg, some ten years previously. It is civil servants like Jasper, who only spring into prominence when they are kidnapped, who do such a wonderful job for Britain either in the Commonwealth or abroad, and who nowadays do it on a shoestring. Unfortunately their work, being generally unknown, goes unsung and unregarded by most people at home. Among other things, we paid our second visit to Expo', visited Mayor Drapeau, and I was interviewed on French language television.

The next port of call was Newfoundland. We stayed at Government House, which had been built by a Cochrane, a member of my grandmother's family. We found that people of our age were furiously British and rather anti-Canadian. If they could afford it they sent their children to school in Britain, pleading that Toronto was nearly as far away as London! But coming from Northern Ireland one of the things which astonished me was the Newfoundland Orange Order. The passage of time had changed it from what it must originally have been into a forward looking organisation of great responsibility.

Sitting next to a prominent member of the Order at a function, I asked him whether they had a charity. He replied that they ran a cancer hospital in St Johns. When I asked whether it was reserved for members of the Order or whether it was open to all Protestants, he astonished me by saying that it was, of course, open for Roman Catholics. He then told me the following story. It was, he said, normal for the Grandmaster of the Order to call at the hospital on Sunday morning and see who would like to be taken to church. As the least fortunate members of society in St Johns tended to be Roman Catholics, he had himself, when Grandmaster, frequently taken Roman Catholics to their church, helped them into their pews and then attended Mass with them.

I was sorry that leading members of the Orange Order in Northern Ireland could not be there to hear his remarks. I have often thought since that if only the Order in Ulster had developed in the same way as the Order in Newfoundland then today's troubles might never have taken place.

One final weekend with the Duponts at Wilmington, which also meant travelling back to New York on Sunday. A final TV appearance on the 'Today Show' in New York and back home from the last official American trip we were to experience.

Having visited America so frequently I can truthfully say that I suffer none of the anti-American feelings which afflict, if only subconsciously, so many British people. I have come to know them and to like them and to feel that we are really the same people. This is what makes me suffer from a split personality when people talk about the Common Market. The people I admire most in politics and in Whitehall are in favour of Britain's entry into EEC. But for purely emotional reasons I often feel attracted to the idea of a union of the English speaking peoples. I believe myself that it will take place by the end of the century and it will include America, Canada, Australia and New Zealand. But Britain will, I suppose, be outside. It is sad to contemplate.

On our return from America we had not long to wait before the balloon went up. On Saturday, 5 October there was a second Civil Rights march. After their first march they had been criticised for lack of publicity by the *Irish Times*. On this occasion they made their plans and saw to it that the media were well briefed in advance. Left-wing MPs from Westminster were invited to attend, and Gerry Fitt, then Republican MP for West Belfast, appeared on the front page of the *Observer* with blood streaming down his head. The Civil Rights movement had arrived. Needless to say, one of our Trade Weeks, this time in Leicester, was starting on Monday and so we were flying to London on Sunday to catch the train to Leicester. It wasn't exactly a good send-off.

The normal pattern for the opening day of these Ulster Weeks was for Jean and I to make a tour of as many shops as possible which were featuring Ulster goods. On every floor of every shop in Leicester I was overtaken by reporters, some with notebooks, others with tape recorders, who wanted interviews on what I thought of the present situation. The shopkeepers who had thrown so much into this Ulster promotion were not amused, and I have a particular memory of seeing a reporter half hidden by a forest of ladies' underwear who emerged as we finished admiring a display of Ulster's best lingerie!

Just as I was about to speak at the official lunch, given by the Lord Mayor, I was told that the Home Secretary wanted me on the telephone. I declined to take the call and ruin the Lord Mayor's lunch. At the end of the meal I was given the following message: 'The House of Lords happens to be sitting today and a special notice question on Northern Ireland will have to be answered. The Government spokesman intends to say that the Prime Minister will be inviting you to Downing Street.' I was glad that I had not left the luncheon table in order to receive this message. The Lord Mayor, Alderman Kenneth Bowden, was a brick throughout the whole day, and supported me at every material moment when I most needed it. I had a curious presentiment during the meal, not only that this would be the last Trade Week which I would attend, but also that it could well be the last time the Red Hand of Ulster would be displayed all over a British city. I was wrong—but only just.

As I had always intended to retire in the autumn of 1969, when I would have been Prime Minister for six and a half years, there was, of course, a natural temptation to go then after five and a half years. By British standards I had then done a respectable stint—under six years—about the same period as Harold Wilson. My policy had been to try and improve community relations, despite the albatross of a reluctant Party hanging round my neck. But if now we were going to have Civil Rights marches and fights in the streets, obviously my policy of trying to improve community relations had received such a severe setback that you could really say it was lying in pieces in the gutter. But of course whenever I hinted at what was in my mind, I was immediately told that it was my duty to stay 'and see this thing through'. I even saw these views expressed in public. For instance, on the evening of 14 October a letter appeared in the *Belfast Telegraph* headed 'Only Captain O'Neill can save an explosive situation.' It was written by a Southern Irishman who had lived in Northern Ireland for six years and in his letter he stated—'He is the only figure who gets any measure of respect from the minority, while at the same time he is, albeit uneasily, accepted by the Unionists as their leader.' It was expressions of opinion such as these which forced me to soldier on despite my opinion that I would be unlikely to achieve anything now in the face of the forces which had been unleashed.

Because Northern Ireland has a government and parliament of its own, dressed up with all the parliamentary designations suitable to a dominion in 1920, the people of Northern Ireland have the greatest difficulty in understanding the limitation of the Government's powers and even more of its finances. At about this time I had the following conversation with a well-meaning Methodist clergyman:

CLERGYMAN: Prime Minister, I have a solution for our problems.
SELF: Please tell me.
CLERGYMAN: We should become a province of Scotland where our problems would be understood.
SELF: We are talking in an agricultural area. Who, for instance, would pay our agricultural subsidies?
CLERGYMAN: Surely the farmer gets paid by Stormont.
SELF: Yes, but the money comes from London.
CLERGYMAN: (Incredulously) But I know a farmer who gets his payments from Stormont.
SELF: Yes, but Stormont can only pay because we are financed from London. This is why the South of Ireland cannot afford our agricultural subsidies.
CLERGYMAN: (Astonished) Well so many of our Protestants are

Presbyterians, perhaps the General Assembly of the Church of Scotland would support us financially.

Presumably this man had a university degree and yet he could not understand Northern Ireland's utter dependence on Westminster. How, then, can the brick-hurling hooligan in a back-street of Belfast begin to understand the situation. The truth of the matter is that the vast majority of the people of Northern Ireland take all our UK advantages for granted and cannot believe that they are at risk. Keep out of our affairs and give us some more money is unfortunately a common Ulster attitude.

The visit to Downing Street, suggested by the Prime Minister while I was in Leicester early in October, was due to take place early in November. The delay might give time for passions to cool. It might also make it possible for the Ulster Government to present its own proposals when we went to London. Several meetings were held, much was discussed, but we will now have to wait till the Ulster Cabinet conclusions are published to see who were in favour of reform, and who were dragging their feet.

At this point of time I should, I think, explain the political situation which existed at that time and which was well known to most intelligent political observers in Northern Ireland. There were two aspirants for the premiership. One was Brian Faulkner, an able and dedicated politician. The other was Bill Craig, who had gradually changed from a forward looking person, interested in continental and international affairs, into a narrow-minded sectarian. He was able to see after the 1966 conspiracy that Faulkner had the right wing of the party behind him and knew that had Faulkner then had the courage to resign he would probably have become Prime Minister and formed a right wing Cabinet. Craig was determined that next time a crisis arose he would have the right wing behind him. By the autumn of 1968 Craig had captured the support which Faulkner had had in 1966. Relationships were not very good between the two, so it was interesting to see that Faulkner was speaking in Craig's constituency. According to the *Belfast Telegraph* on 23 October, Faulkner, then Minister of Commerce, said at a large Unionist meeting, 'We might have to fight to maintain the constitution at some time in the future. I believe there is enough fight left in the people of Ulster to maintain both the political and economic situation of the country.' At the same meeting Craig is quoted as saying: 'I would deal firmly with anyone inside or outside Ulster who would try to undermine the constitution.'

There was, however, one bright spot. Earlier the Cabinet had agreed that I could call a meeting of local authorities to discuss how house building could be speeded up, and I announced this when the House resumed on 15 October. This meeting took place on 30 October and there I stressed the need for a fair allocation of houses. I was warned that extreme Unionists who did not like to see Catholics getting houses in the local areas which they controlled, and extreme National-ists who didn't like seeing Protestants getting houses in areas they controlled, would be highly displeased, but I ignored this advice. I further went on to ask for a points system to be introduced for the allocation of houses as in Britain. The repercussions from this were far greater than I could have anticipated.

For the first time for many years Derry had a mayor who was not a politician. He was, in fact, a retired school-teacher who had some-what reluctantly assumed the mayor's duties in this unhappy city. He rose and welcomed my remarks, saying that if houses could be allo-cated on a recognised system it would get Derry out of a difficult problem. From this point we moved on to the abolition of the Derry Corporation. Without the co-operation and help of this courageous man, this, the greatest of the reforms which I was able to achieve, would have been impossible. How often in history have compromise candidates achieved far more than someone who has worked hard to achieve his life's ambition. Pope John himself is a case in point. Today, responsible Protestants in Londonderry are perfectly happy with their Commission from whom they get fair local government, and the Catholics, who are the majority, are glad to see the removal of minority local government administration. Had the Commission been in existence years before and had sufficient houses been provided on an impartial basis, Derry would not have provided the dry tinder which lit the explosion which nearly engulfed the Province in August 1969.

Soon after the Housing Conference at the end of October, I travelled to London for the Downing Street meeting. The following morning I met Brian Faulkner and Bill Craig who had travelled over to London by separate early planes, and we went through the notes that I had brought with me. By their joint decision we went naked into the Cabinet Room. In the end, of course, they were forced to agree to a package of reforms. It would, however, have been more dignified if we had been able to make our own proposals.

On our return a large number of Cabinet meetings were required before a five point package of reforms could be agreed. The back-ground to all these proceedings were continual Civil Rights demonstrations and continual Paisleyite protests, with Craig playing the role of the only—or nearly the only—man in the Cabinet who could 'save Ulster'. At this time Chichester-Clark, a retired regular soldier, who was living at and farming his ancestral home, limited himself to about one Cabinet meeting a week. Enquiries produced the reply that he was busy either in his Ministry (Agriculture) or on his own farm. Craig, noticing these absences, proposed to him that they should both resign. Doubtless he reckoned that this would be a very quick route to the premiership. However, his suggestions produced exactly the opposite results from those which he had anticipated, and Jimmy Chichester-Clark, who had previously muttered about bringing in reforms under duress, was now galvanised into action. From that moment on, with his previous experience as Chief Whip, he played a leading part in ensuring that we could put a package of reforms together. I feel I must mention this small episode. It is, of course, well known that Jimmy brought me down, by going back on a Cabinet decision about the introduction of 'one man, one vote' and voting against this reform at the Party meeting which introduced it. What has hitherto never been revealed is the part he played in introducing our earliest 'Civil Rights' reforms. Maybe it was Craig's proposals which galvanised him into action, but at this distance of time credit should be given where credit is due.

I have often wondered since whether there was any way in which I could have brought home the seriousness of the situation as I then saw it, both to those of my colleagues who were living in the past, or to the right wing of the Party. But supposing I had been invested with the power of being able to foretell the future, would anyone have listened?

There we were in November 1968, the activities of the Civil Rights movement appeared to the Party to be nearly treasonable. Supposing I had spoken as follows: 'This, gentlemen, is a mere picnic to what you may expect next summer. Then there will be such appalling rioting, arson, death and destruction that the British Army will be brought to the aid of the exhausted police force. When this happens Stormont will virtually lose control over its own affairs. Mr Callaghan will come over to Belfast with the head of the London Police at his side and a packet of reforms in his pocket. You, gentlemen, will then be faced with doing what Westminster requires, or risking the possibility of the suspension of the Northern Ireland Government. Moreover, for the first time in Northern Ireland's history a UK representative of ambassadorial rank will be stationed in Stormont

Castle, which will certainly be a strange anomaly for an integral part of the United Kingdom.'

Had I made such remarks either at a Cabinet meeting or at a party meeting, I would have been laughed to scorn, and yet that, and much else, was to take place only ten short months after we were wrangling over this small, timid reform package.

As soon as the reforms had been agreed by the Cabinet, the Parliamentary Party had to be consulted. This was achieved without too much difficulty, but some ten days had to elapse before a wider party meeting had to endorse the reforms. Craig, perhaps surprised by the ease with which the Parliamentary Party had endorsed the proposals, used the intervening period to make strong old fashioned Unionist speeches to delirious crowds. He doubtless hoped that the wider Party meeting would chuck them out. But, in fact, they also endorsed them.

After a quiet weekend I made a broadcast on television on Monday evening, 9 December.* Little did I realise the impact that this would have. It was announced on Sunday night and again on Monday morning that I would be 'speaking to the nation'. Employers encouraged their workers to go home early so that they could watch it, and after it was over I had the equivalent, by British standards, of five million messages of support. But before the full impact had been felt, Craig—who was then going to a Unionist meeting every night—criticised my TV appearance. I sent for him at nine o'clock the following morning, Wednesday, 11 December and sacked him.

Once or twice I had made him drop a proposed paragraph from a speech, which seemed to me almost to propose UDI. I brought out these—as I considered them—dangerous tendencies in our public exchange of letters. But I could not forget the old days when we had been close friends, and so I concluded my letter by writing: 'I am sorry to have to say this, for we have been colleagues for over five years and friends for a longer time.' In actual fact, our friendship had been very strained for many months. After he left more and more stories came to me of how he had been trying to undermine my position ever since the Civil Rights demonstrations had started, but it would be pointless to rake over these ashes today.

However, what can be mentioned at this distance in time is his conduct as a minister. Frequently during his term of office I was called upon to defend his conduct. Early during his ministerial career he suggested that the trades unions should take 'a running jump off a great height'. On one occasion I can remember being rung up at one

---

* The full text of my broadcast is included as Appendix I.

of the large London railway stations to be told that his conduct in the House had offended many people and that I must return at once to deal with the criticism. He was a man of great charm who had a fatal fluency of speech. He enjoyed stepping on to a platform in a large hall and receiving a tumultuous welcome. Not for him the more difficult role of warning the Unionist audiences that unless they adopted a reasonable attitude the whole future of Northern Ireland might be in doubt. When I asked for his resignation it was obvious to everyone that I had no choice. Perhaps I should have parted with him earlier, but I doubt whether the course of Northern Ireland's history would have been any different in the end.

Meanwhile, for the remainder of that week support continued to pour in from all quarters and in retrospect I feel I should really have called an election. Had I done so I believe a large number of extremists would have lost their seats. But there were two reasons why such a course would have been impossible at that time. First of all, I had actually stated in my broadcast that it would be wrong to hold an election. Secondly, Christmas was upon us. In these matters it is so easy to be wise after the event, but as in the end an election was forced upon the Cabinet the following February, it would have been far wiser to have gone to the country then.

Not only was that week passed with incredible and almost unanimous support at home, but leaders appeared in all the national papers in full support. One, written in the *Daily Express* on Tuesday, 10 December, ended as follows: 'Let the words of a famous Irishman, Edmund Burke, be recalled in Ulster today: "When bad men combine the good must associate; else they will fall, one by one, an unpitied sacrifice in a contemptible struggle."' Those words were prophetic for us, not only because my successor survived for only one year and ten months, but because other good men and true have also fallen by the wayside. That autumn Dick Ferguson won the constituency of South Antrim by a record majority. I went and spoke for him at a rowdy meeting and was kicked on the shins as I left the hall. He was eventually forced out of his seat by bully boy tactics and when he had resigned a bomb was exploded in his front garden. He was the most liberal supporter I had. In the autumn of 1970 Bertie Porter, who I made Minister of Home Affairs early in 1969, had to resign, partly for personal reasons, but also because of the insults which he and his family suffered at the hands of hooligans.

The Civil Rights movement called off all their marches. The leader of the Nationalist Party, Eddie McAteer, rang me up the night after the broadcast to congratulate me. A Parliamentary Party meeting on the Thursday following my TV appearance was a walk-over. I insisted on having a vote of confidence in me personally as otherwise there would only have been a unanimous vote of support for the Government. As a result I managed to get four people to abstain. They were all extremists and included Harry West, whom Brian Faulkner later included in his Cabinet.

My wife's family insisted that we should come over to their home on the Solent for Christmas. This we did. While there I made some notes of all that had happened since October, and became convinced that unless the Unionist Party could change its attitude—which in essence is expressed by Paisley when he says 'we will be masters in our own house'—we were heading for disaster. It was also obvious that unless there could be some reconciliation between the two sections of the community then we might well find ourselves without a house to be masters in. For if disorder continued then clearly London would become involved. However, even though I could feel sure that this was what the future held, I must admit that I did not appreciate that it was only eight months before British troops would be forced to come to the aid of the civil power for the first time for thirty-five years. For me personally it was a peaceful close to a difficult year. Northern Ireland had certainly hit the headlines, but curiously enough, as I shall seek to show in the next chapter, I still continued to enjoy massive support among the minority. They had seen photographs of me visiting Catholic schools, sitting beside their Cardinal at a ceremony in Armagh, visiting Catholic hospitals, greeting Prime Ministers of the Republic at Stormont, making conciliatory speeches. While they knew that I was in favour of staying within the UK they also knew that I wanted good community relations. They also knew that I was utterly opposed to any idea of a master race in Northern Ireland. Whatever might, or might not, be allowed to happen in South Africa—an independent country outside the United Kingdom —it would be ludicrous to suggest that such a policy could be viable inside the UK, even if one could have squared it with one's conscience, which I certainly could not.

One further small item is worthy of mention. That brave Methodist Minister, the Rev Eric Lallaher, arranged for the Nationalist Party leader, Eddie McAteer and myself to appear together on television at Christmas time and read passages from the Bible. Yet another effort on his part to show the people of Northern Ireland that we are all Christians.

12

 Before Resignation

AFTER the TV appearance before Christmas, the Civil Rights movement called off all their marches—at least till the end of January. There was, however, an extreme left-wing element which had jumped on to the Civil Rights bandwagon. Based on the Queen's University of Belfast, they called themselves the 'People's Democracy'. They were determined to break the Civil Rights truce, and break it they did. They celebrated the New Year by marching from Belfast to Derry. The police felt that if a ban were imposed then a very small group of people would turn into a large rabble with yet another grievance. However, even assuming that this interpretation was correct, the events along the route of the march were so violent that the Christmas spirit of peace was completely shattered.

After Christmas I travelled to Newcastle upon Tyne to be interviewed by Ludovic Kennedy for the Tyne-Tees programme called 'Face the Press'. While waiting to go on the programme I was informed of the police decision on the PD march. I then rang the Minister of Home Affairs to check whether he agreed with it. As usual in such matters—and it must be remembered that in those days there was no army involvement—any decision about a march was a finely balanced exercise. The element in this decision which worried me most was that there was a hint that strong Protestant opposition might stop the march *en route*, perhaps in Antrim, some sixteen miles away. In the event the police ferried them round Antrim and the next morning round the next town, Randalstown. What had started as a pathetic, bedraggled, left-wing, long-haired walk, whose members, had they only been left alone, would have limped into Londonderry after a four day march, was gradually making headlines as Protestant opposition built up.

On the second day of the march, Thursday, 2 January, I was keen to come home, but as always on these occasions, I was advised not to make a hasty return in case it should be misinterpreted. From the predominantly Protestant town of Randalstown, outside my old home at Shanes Castle, to the Catholic village of Toomebridge, they passed through the southern tip of my constituency, Bannside. Then when they had crossed the Bann they arrived in the constituency of Major Chichester-Clark. I have no doubt whatsoever that this was all carefully planned on an *agent provocateur* basis. Two people leapt to fame as a result of the march, Bernadette Devlin and Michael Farrell. In the February election one month later Farrell stood against me presumably in order to try to take the Catholic vote away from me and let Paisley win the seat. It was a little plan which went wrong, and I've often been told since that extreme Catholics voted for Paisley on the argument that if you could put Paisley into Parliament you would put Harold Wilson into Belfast.

Across the Bann Bernadette Devlin stood against Major Chichester-Clark, and while she was beaten, she laid the foundations for her victory in Mid-Ulster a few months later. It was this march which blew her from obscurity as an unknown university student into fame and Westminster. The struggles across the Bann ensured a flat in Belgravia, a sports car and several visits to America!

But to get back to this fateful march on Friday, 3 January, I insisted on returning home. On Saturday morning, 4 January, I had a telephone call at 11 a.m. from my old friend Robin Chichester-Clark. To my surprise he told me that he and his brother had been watching the march through their constituencies. He then asked me to go on the Northern Ireland sound 'News' just before lunch and announce that I had ordered out the 'B' Specials. He said that he and his brother both felt that unless this were done the Protestant backlash would be too dreadful to contemplate. I flatly refused. I said I would resign before I did any such thing. Not even the police had made this suggestion, let alone any member of the Cabinet. I have never regretted this decision.

Very soon after this telephone call the marchers were ambushed at Burntollet Bridge outside Derry. It was the sort of thing which everyone had been fearing would happen and it provided a very unpleasant finale to a very unpleasant march. Any liberal-minded person must admit that the Civil Rights movements brought about reforms which would otherwise have taken years to wring from a reluctant Government. It is also beyond question that the riots of August 1969 completely changed the course of Northern Ireland's future, but I doubt whether the history books will show that the 'People's Democracy' played a useful role in the advancement of necessary reforms.

For some years a Dublin paper, the *Sunday Independent*, had been carrying a Christmas poll entitled 'The Man of the Year'. The day after the march finished, on Sunday, 5 January, the headline in that newspaper read, 'O'Neill is Irish Man of the Year'. Two things were interesting about the figures. First, 90 per cent of my support came from South of the border. Secondly, the Cardinal came fourth, one place ahead of Jack Lynch. Doubtless the television appearance before Christmas had had a lot to do with it, but nevertheless it was a bit surprising. Mr De Valera came twenty-first on the list. Could anyone ever have forecast that one day a Prime Minister of Northern Ireland would beat the President of the Irish Republic in a popularity contest held in Dublin! It showed just how much the even keel of Irish life had been upset since the start of the Civil Rights movement.

On 9 January we flew to London. That night there was a reception for the Commonwealth Prime Ministers at Lancaster House. I had decided that the time had come to explain to the Government and to the Leader of the Opposition how serious the situation was becoming. Ever since the first Civil Rights march had taken place in October 1968, and fighting in the streets had become the order of the day, I felt that my policy of trying to improve relations between the two sections of the community was lying in pieces on the floor. I could not really see how I could continue in office under such conditions. I hoped I would be able to make London understand. Little did I know what awaited me.

First I went to the Albany for lunch with the Leader of the Opposition. As usual on these occasions I found the meal, the company and the conversation most agreeable. When, however, I brought the conversation round to the necessity for my early political retirement I met a blank wall. He would not hear of it. When I persisted in my remarks he talked about my duty, adding for good measure that if I went I would be succeeded either by a crook or a lunatic!

Ken Bloomfield came to collect me from the Albany and as he was ringing the bell of the Heath flat I was being asked what I would do if I retired. Would I retire to my family place? I explained that as a younger son I had no place to which I could retire. 'Well then,' he said, 'you must soldier on.' With Ken's arrival I retired to wash and then we all set off down the 'Rope Walk' to the front door of the Albany where many photographers were waiting. Then on to the

Home Office, but in the car Ken told me that Heath had pressed him to stop me resigning. I had never been as friendly with Jim Callaghan as I had been with Roy Jenkins. This was not only because, perhaps, I had more in common with Roy, but also because I felt that if I visited Callaghan too often I might find myself in difficulties with Harold Wilson. In any case, if I had expected that Jim Callaghan would quietly acquiesce to my proposed resignation I was greatly mistaken. His attitude was one of, 'You must be joking. I know, you've just come here to blow off.' In a different way he was just as aghast as Ted had been earlier.

That night Jean and I went to Lancaster House for the Commonwealth Prime Ministers' reception. My knowledge of these Prime Ministers was now getting slender. Harold Holt, whom I had known for many years, was dead. Lester Pearson, who had received us in Ottawa, had retired. However I soon ran into Mitchell Sharp, a prominent member of the Liberal Government in Canada who was an old friend, and as his wife had Ulster origins he was interested and worried about the future of Northern Ireland. He was no less concerned when I had finished explaining the situation to him. It is strange how through all the various functions I attended, sometimes in the midst of serious crises, I can still remember some of the details of what occurred. From Mitchell Sharp I remember running into another redhead—Paul Johnson of journalistic fame. He forecast in quiet tones that I would go down as the most famous Irishman in history. I asked why. 'Because', he replied, 'you will soon be assassinated and then you will be canonised by Dublin!' Up to the moment of writing his forecast has not yet proved true. I remember introducing Ted Heath to Matt Busby, and then, when I was beginning to wonder when the party would be likely to end, I was touched on the shoulder by a Secretary from No 10. 'Could you please stay in this room, near this spot and I will shepherd the Prime Minister in your direction.' He soon arrived. 'You're not going to let us down, Terence, I'm sure, are you? You were merely trying to frighten Jim, weren't you? Come and have lunch tomorrow.' I declined the invitation, not only for the good reason that we were returning on the morning plane, but also because I really couldn't face any more London pressure for me to stay on.

It is interesting to recall that at this time Mr Faulkner, still Minister of Commerce for another fortnight, was warning the country that any more disorder would make the attraction of new industry very difficult. At one stage in an interview with the *Belfast News*

Letter he said, 'But I must point out that there have been cases where companies have gone slow in their talks with us, simply as a result of tension.' He also talked about the initial serious disturbances in Londonderry. Later that year what happened in Londonderry and Belfast was to make this Civil Rights period seem like a picnic. On many occasions in the past two years the Government of Northern Ireland have given hopeful reviews of the industrial situation. I wonder how much truth there was in these reviews?

About this time also I brought a new MP into the Government, Bertie Porter—one of the last members for Queen's University (University representation was to be abolished at the next election) —as a Parliamentary Secretary in Home Affairs. Although he had only been an MP for a very short time, he had entered Parliament specifically to support my policies. In a short time he was to become Minister of Home Affairs where he played a loyal and distinguished part. He stayed on, after some hesitation, with my successor, resigning in the autumn of 1970, when he received a well-deserved knighthood. It is tragic that he did not come to Stormont sooner as he would have been a valuable member of the administration, though one of the problems is that the low salaries paid to Ministers in Northern Ireland makes it hard for someone like a lawyer to give up his practice for any length of time.

A week after my return from London we announced the setting up of a Commission of Enquiry. Various hurdles, some of them legal, had to be surmounted before the announcement could be made. One of these was a lengthy Cabinet meeting. The terms of reference of this Enquiry (known as the Cameron Commission, after its Chairman, the distinguished judge, Lord Cameron of the Scottish High Court) were as follows: 'To enquire into and report on the course of events leading to, and the immediate causes and nature of the violence and civil disturbances in Northern Ireland on and since 5 October 1968; and to assess the composition, conduct and aims of those bodies involved in the current agitation and in any incidents arising out of it.'

Over a week after the Cabinet decision, Brian Faulkner resigned because of the Cabinet decision to set up the enquiry. He was hastily followed by another Cabinet minister, his evangelical friend, Billy Morgan. The latter fence-sitting minister's resignation was almost a relief. Looking back, however, it is interesting to see whether the public reasons Faulkner gave for his resignation have stood the test of time. His main stated reason was that the setting up of the

Cameron Commission was a political manoeuvre.* I think historians will agree that this commission, whose institution was welcomed by both the Prime Minister and the Leader of Opposition at Westminster, performed a useful service. Among other findings, Lord Cameron stated in no uncertain terms that there had been discrimination in Northern Ireland. This was one of the things which annoyed the Unionist Party so far as I was concerned. I had also said this in public. I remember watching Ian Waller of the *Sunday Telegraph* and Brian Faulkner on television in earlier days. Faulkner was defending with enthusiasm the indefensible Londonderry situation. This was the faithful Party line which Cameron blew sky high.

Faulkner, who is a very able politician, went on television after his resignation and projected a very liberal image. I was, however, not the only person to be surprised by this performance, especially with regard to the issue of one man one vote for the local government franchise. It was the denial of this principle in Derry city which he had so vigorously defended in the Ian Waller interview.

Shortly before the autumn visit to Downing Street I had received three Protestant clergymen who wanted to express the hope that we would make suggestions for reforms which could be carried out in the ensuing months. I was accompanied by Faulkner at this meeting. One of the three ministers was a leading Presbyterian, the Reverend Professor J. R. Boyd, and he was so astonished by the post-resignation TV performance that he sent me the following letter:

Dear Prime Minister,

Immediately after the appearance of Mr Faulkner on BBC TV on Friday last, and his reference to his long-held views on universal local franchise, I felt it my duty to write to remind him of the interview, granted by you and him to Archdeacon Mercer, Reverend David Turtle and me, at Stormont in the afternoon of 29 *October 1968*.

In my letter I pointed out that, on that occasion it was *he* who argued strongly in favour of a ratepayers' vote on the same lines as in Canada etc. It was *he* who assured us that on the forthcoming visit to London there was 'nothing here of which anyone needed to be ashamed'.

While not wishing to make public what took place at a private interview, I want to remind you of it, and of the date, so that

* The full text of the letters between myself and Brian Faulkner at the time of his resignation on 23 January 1969 are given in Appendix II.

you may make such use of this information as you feel appropriate.

I must add that I share the desire of all to whom I speak that you may feel able to hold fast as Prime Minister and give the strong lead to which the mass of our people will respond as you proceed with all those liberal policies which can make our Province indeed 'a respected part of the United Kingdom'.

Yours faithfully,
James R. Boyd.

Faulkner is a Presbyterian and I am an Anglican: it is therefore of some significance, in Northern Ireland terms, that I should ever have received this letter. On this date in January 1969 so much had happened since 29 October 1968 that I had overlooked the interview with the Protestant clergy. I was glad to be reminded of it and as suggested in the letter I showed it to my colleagues and their remarks on reading it were not the sort which one can put in print!

Shortly after the report of the Cameron Commission was published I was talking to a Church of Ireland (Anglican) clergyman. It was several months after my resignation. 'Do you know,' he said, 'I always thought the word "discrimination" was part of Nationalist propaganda until I read the Cameron report. Now I realise more clearly than ever what you were trying to do.' If Lord Cameron had done no more than open the eyes of a typical, decent Anglican clergyman, brave, moderate but uninformed, he would have performed a useful service. In fact, of course, he did far more. His report became one of the text books upon which reform could be based.

I shall not be alive when they are published, but I reiterate that I will be content to be judged by the Cabinet conclusions of the meetings of the Northern Ireland Cabinet which took place between October 1968 and Faulkner's resignation, and indeed on up to my own resignation on 1 May 1969.

While on the subject of Cabinet conclusions, I should mention that a new Governor, Lord Grey of Naunton, had been appointed in the autumn of 1968. Shortly after his appointment he suggested that as the Queen's representative he should see a copy of the Cabinet conclusions as was the practice in London. I readily agreed that this should be done, so a copy of the conclusions rests today not only at Stormont Castle, but also at Government House!

Faulkner's other reason for resignation was his suggestion that he had always been in favour of one man one vote. Why then, I wonder, did he so vigorously defend the Derry situation on television? No one in Northern Ireland who can remember the Faulkner of 1968 would connect his name with reform, certainly not with political reform which might rectify the justifiable grievances of the minority.

One further point, while I am dealing with the Faulkner resignation. Shortly before I sacked Bill Craig I told Brian that I was increasingly worried about Craig's behaviour. I always remember his Freudian reply. 'Of course Bill has got the Party sewn up from the extreme right to the centre.' This had been Faulkner's original strength within the Party. Had I realised it, he was, in fact, telling me that having lost his original supporters to Craig, he must now somehow get hold of mine. This, in the end, was what he did—but only two years after I had left the scene and only because they thought he might be the only man who could save the Stormont system.

To fill Faulkner's resignation as Minister of Commerce, I appointed Roy Bradford. Bertie Porter took Morgan's place as Minister of Health and Social Services.

The headlines during the next few days seemed to show that I was surviving far too well for the liking of the right-wing extremists. 'Majority still back O'Neill'—*Belfast News Letter*, 28 January. 'O'Neill wins vote in Stormont debate'—*Irish Times,* 30 January. As a result thirteen back-benchers asked for a Party meeting. It was 1966 all over again, but with a difference. By this time Faulkner, who had failed to resign at the time of 'the conspiracy', had now resigned.

But perhaps in retrospect the most prophetic comment in the press was made by *The Times* on 25 January. At the end of their leader devoted to Faulkner they said:

His resignation and call for 'strong Government' is the most acute threat to Captain O'Neill's position yet to develop. The Cabinet and the Party at Stormont with whom it lies either to confirm or turn aside that threat, have a duty to weigh well what Captain O'Neill's fall could mean for civil peace in Ulster and for its constitutional relationship with Westminster.

All members of the Government issued a statement of support and as in all previous crises, messages started to pour in to Stormont Castle. On Sunday morning, 2 February, Jean and I drove from Stormont House to Belfast Cathedral for morning service. We were astonished when the Dean devoted his sermon to the political crises and warned of the grim future which might arise if I and my policies were overturned. Little did I or the congregation realise that his prophecies would be fulfilled in August, seven months later.

The next day, Monday, 3 February, I called increasing numbers of Ministers in for discussions until we had assembled the whole Cabinet. We were aware that twelve back-benchers were assembling in a hotel in Portadown in order to get publicity prior to the Party meeting which they were demanding. This became known in Northern Ireland as the 'Portadown Parliament'.

During the course of the day more and more Ministers decided that the gauntlet which this 'Parliament' was in the process of throwing down must be picked up. In the end there was one doubter—Jimmy Chichester-Clark. Coming up to six o'clock we adjourned up to the Conference Room at Stormont Castle which I had created when the Castle was modernised in 1963. In it there was a television set and on it we watched the results of the 'Portadown Parliament'. The arrogance of the performers made all of us quite determined to visit Government House that night and ask for a dissolution.

There is one vital difference between the practice at Westminster and that in Northern Ireland on these occasions. Whereas in London it is the prerogative of the Prime Minister to advise the Queen to dissolve Parliament, in Belfast the Governor can only dissolve Parliament on the advice of his ministers. Former senior civil servants have told me that in Lord Craigavon's day this constitutional point was more honoured in the breach than in the observance. Indeed, I believe on one occasion his entire Cabinet read of the impending election in the evening paper! But on this particular occasion it seemed to me that we had to act as a united Cabinet. And while, in fact, we were overwhelmingly in favour of going to the country, by about 5 p.m. any lingering doubts were dispelled by the television news.

When various formalities had been completed we set off later that evening to Government House, where the Governor quite properly asked whether this was a unanimous decision. I was about to reply when to my astonishment a minister who in the morning had been hesitant replied that we were all of one mind. That settled it. Later it became clear to me why earlier that day Chichester-Clark had not been keen on an election. When he went before his delegates for reselection he was only chosen by a smallish majority after a fight with an extreme candidate.

The details of the election at this distance of time are not interesting but here are some points which I remember. Inevitably my own campaign in the Bannside constituency suffered, though it got off to a good start. Despite the fact that in the years between 1965 and 1969

I had met Mr Lynch, visited Catholic schools, been photographed with the Cardinal, priests and nuns, and made the sort of speeches which none of my predecessors, or even my then colleagues, had ever made, I was reselected by the Bannside delegates with acclamation. I want at this point to restress this fact. For many people photographs are far more powerful weapons than the printed word. Neither my predecessor nor my successor when he was in office visited a Catholic school or was photographed with priests and nuns. There were many photographs of me with people of this kind, and in which it was apparent that I was enjoying their company. These photographs were burnt from time to time in public. But despite all these disadvantages the delegates of Bannside reselected me by acclamation. That is something I shall always remember, however long and unhappy the future of Northern Ireland may be.

In every other way, however, I fought the election under grave disadvantages. As there had never been a contest in all the years of my membership since 1946, the election machinery was very rusty. This was counteracted to some extent by various factors. The Secretary of the Association, Bertie Vaughan, was highly efficient and gave much of his valuable time for the duration of the contest. The ladies in general, and Ruby McClure in particular, also gave massive assistance.

Apart from the difficulties within the constituency, there were also difficulties outside. The Press of the world had descended on Ulster, and interviews were sought in French and German. Press conferences were required in Belfast and other MPs wanted assistance. One person who gave me his whole time was Henry Clark, still then Member of Parliament for North Antrim at Westminster. He came over from London and worked for us throughout the entire campaign. I have never heard anyone at Westminster say anything against Henry. As the Americans would say, 'He was that kind of a man'.

Patrick, our son, took ten days off from his job in London and worked hard throughout the entire contest. And Jean, who knew and was known throughout the constituency, slaved away through the snow as we canvassed from door to door.

Last, but by no means least, our gardener, Robert Strange, helped us in every way he could. Robert, the very best type of Ulsterman, shrewd, knowledgeable and keenly interested, was to see during those ten days as he drove round Bannside, personalities as diverse as Martin Bell and Auberon Waugh. His television screen is that much more interesting today because he has actually seen these people covering the canvass, tramping through a factory in Cullybackey, or interviewing me as to how I thought things were going.

As I have already remarked, Michael Farrell, one of Bernadette Devlin's revolutionary friends in the 'People's Democracy' movement, probably stood against me for the express purpose of taking Catholic votes away from me and hopefully of letting Paisley in. For at that time among extreme Catholics there was a feeling that if Paisley could be put into Parliament, Wilson would be put into Belfast. After polling day some of the old hands in my constituency reckoned that Paisley had, in fact, got many extreme Catholic votes. If this was true—and I think it probably was—then not only did it show how difficult it was to break down ancient barriers, but also how grim the outlook would be.

During the election, in addition to Henry Clark's sterling work in the constituency, I also heard that another Westminster member, James Hamilton, had given a television interview. In it he stated, to my surprise, that if I was turned out there would be a civil war. Everyone laughed, but August 1969, when five hundred houses were burnt down and ten people shot in the streets, before the British army intervened, in the nick of time, was indeed a civil war situation. It was later than everybody—including myself—realised.

I have two other happy memories of the election. One in Bannside and one in the new constituency of Larkfield. In my constituency there is a small village called Dunloy. It is 90 per cent Catholic. We were doing our usual canvass and getting a good reception when I was told that a large gathering awaited me at the cross-roads. As is the way in Ulster elections, I had a small loudspeaker van and it was covered with Union Jacks. As they all wanted me to address them I had to get out of my car and fight my way to the van. There, surrounded by Union Jacks, I addressed this cheering Catholic crowd. This incident, meaningless to the average Englishman, is full of memories for me. It shows what might have been possible if extremists had not insisted on committing suicide in public. My friends told me that the Catholic 'People's Democracy' candidate, Michael Farrell, rushed to Dunloy to try and turn the population against me. There are those who say he succeeded to some extent. But there was one other reason why the reception I received from the Catholics was incredible. Their only industry, a local abattoir, had been closed by the Government a week before.

The other incident took place in the new shopping area at Andersonstown, a name not unfamiliar to those who watch their television screens today. This Roman Catholic area, with extensive new housing estates, was in the new constituency of Larkfield on the outskirts of

Belfast. The Unionist, or Protestant, majority in the constituency was only three or four hundred. The candidate, Basil McIvor, was decent, moderate, but unknown. Obviously he would be a useful addition to the Party, and obviously he was worthy of Catholic support. One afternoon I met him in the constituency and together we drove to Andersonstown where, after four months of the Civil Rights movement, I wondered what my reception would be like. When we arrived I expected to have to say a few words, but when I saw the vast crowd and the lack of a microphone I merely squeezed out of the car. I was immediately surrounded by people. Everyone either wanted to shake me by the hand or slap me on the back. Andersonstown has since become famous for riots and troop searches where no Ulster ministers would be welcome, but Basil McIvor got in with a majority of some six thousand.

Had the Catholics throughout the Province voted like that all the pro-O'Neill candidates, as they were called, would have been returned and a rejuvenated and reformed Unionist Party would have been returned to Stormont. The Catholics would have been given new heart to see that moderation actually paid off and produced dividends, while the Protestant extremists would have been horrified to see that if you wanted to win a seat you had to pay some attention to the moderate vote. But it was not to be. The disappointing result of this election was one of the reasons why the terrible riots of August 1969 took place.

Some years after Northern Ireland came into existence, the west of the province was gerrymandered by the first Government of Northern Ireland. When the British ruled Ireland the counties of Fermanagh and Tyrone had Nationalist—that is, Catholic—majorities which provided for them control of local Government. And even on a householders' franchise, which favoured the Protestants, the Catholics had won control of Derry City for a brief moment in the early 1920s. But the whole thing was wrested from their hands and left in the control of families like the Brookes in Fermanagh. Understandably the Catholics in West Ulster never forgot or forgave. It was in West Ulster that the pro-O'Neill candidates did worst. In the East there were some astonishing results. In Larne Bill Craig should have had a majority of some fifteen thousand as the official Unionist candidate. In fact, he scraped in with a majority of six hundred against the popular pro-O'Neill local surgeon who kept on saying, 'I am not a politician and I cannot make speeches', or words to that effect! In North Derry the extremist candidate got in with a majority of some one hundred votes after a recount.

My colleagues in the Cabinet pressed me to stay on. A lot of clever people produced figures to show how well we had done; but I knew in my bones that the game was up. In a month's time I would have been Prime Minister for six years. Quite a respectable stint even by British standards. Why should I soldier on in this impossible situation? In fact, but for certain events in April it is quite possible that I would have carried on till the autumn. I am glad that it did not turn out in that way.

One of the many problems facing me was something quite ludicrous. Three pro-O'Neill candidates had won seats. One of these—Major Hall-Thompson—was the son of a former Minister of Education who had been sacked by Lord Brookeborough because his Education Bill, for which Lord Brookeborough voted, was unpopular. Despite his liberal image he was nevertheless an official Unionist in his own constituency, but until his constituency agreed to it, he could not come to Parliamentary Party meetings. He could only vote for me in the House of Commons. There were two other independent pro-O'Neill candidates without strong Unionist backgrounds who defeated the Unionist candidates in their constituencies. Despite the fact that they supported the Government's policies as carried out by Stormont and now dictated by Whitehall, two of them are still, at the moment of writing, outside the Parliamentary Party over two years later. These three votes would have been invaluable at that time at Party meetings but the extremists were determined to keep them out.

The extreme back-benchers set about the job of bringing me down by extra Parliamentary methods and to this end they decided to use the various groupings of the Unionist Party. There was a Standing Committee of between three and four hundred people and a much larger body called the Ulster Unionist Council nominally consisting of some nine hundred people, many of whom never attended. These organisations were hallowed by history and had their roots in the 1912 era and even earlier when Carson visited Ulster—he never lived there—and fought for her rights at Westminster.

Towards the end of March there took place the first of three explosions which quite literally blew me out of office. I had already survived both a Parliamentary Party meeting held immediately after the election, and also a Standing Committee meeting at which I got a two-thirds majority. Obviously someone was keen to influence the voting at this larger gathering of the Ulster Unionist Council. In order to achieve this end a large electricity sub-station on the outskirts of Belfast was blown up before the meeting. It seemed to me that there were two organisations which might be responsible. One was the IRA and the other the extreme Protestant organisation, the Ulster Volunteer Force. If I had had to choose I would have selected the latter as having the greater interest in getting rid of me. It undoubtedly influenced the vote at the meeting where I only got a majority of seventy-five out of an attendance of six hundred. As in so many other countries and organisations, it is the militants who are keen enough to attend meetings. Had another hundred moderates bothered to come the vote would have looked better—though the end result would have been the same.

April 1969, the last month of my premiership, was full of difficulties. I would like, however, to record an incident which showed how hard it was to get people to see the situation with which we were faced. I had myself been protected against Protestant assassination for about two years; though when the police gave me their information and the reasons for the protection, I still refused to have a detective. So instead I was saddled with a small car occupied by two policemen which followed me wherever I went. I was still, even under threat of assassination, the only Prime Minister in Western Europe without a detective from the day I became Prime Minister until the day I resigned over six years later. Obviously, or so it seemed to me, the Protestants had the better reasons for bringing about my departure from the political scene.

With this in mind, one day I was standing on a sunny April morning chatting to a senior police officer. 'Don't', I said, 'put it out of your mind that these explosions may be the work of extreme Protestants.' He looked aghast and his reply was to the effect that loyalists would never destroy their own country. I suggested that it might well be worth their while blowing up the water supply to Belfast if the end result was to bring down the Prime Minister by making the people think that it was all the work of the IRA. In the autumn Protestants were arrested and charged with responsibility for these outrages after an attempt to blow up an electrical installation just across the border had resulted in a man's death; but by then we already had semi-direct rule from London, and Sir Arthur Young, the head of the London police, in charge of the Ulster police. All my predecessors had had detectives to protect them from extreme Catholics, yet despite the fact that their intelligence had found that I was in danger from extreme Protestants two years earlier, this particular officer still imagined that the explosions must be the work of the IRA.

April 1969 was now drawing to a close. Belfast had been without water for a week as a result of two explosions; one in the Mountains of Mourne and the other at Dunadry near the airport where pipes taking water from Lough Neagh were severed. There had also been the aforementioned electricity sub-station explosion at Castlereagh on the outskirts of Belfast. I felt that my time was running out and that I would, before I went, bring in 'one man one vote' for local government elections. In retrospect, it is odd to think that Protestant explosions may have hastened the introduction of this reform. Up to date it had been impossible to get Cabinet agreement to this move—hence the five-point programme before Christmas omitting this vital point.

By the weekend of Saturday, 19 April, the Cabinet had agreed to this move. On Tuesday, 22 April, we were to have a Party meeting, but it came to no conclusion owing to the deliberate verbosity of the extremists. I explained why I supported the Minister of Home Affairs in the decision that we had taken and finished by explaining that if after the Minister, Bertie Porter, had gone into the details, and others in the Party had spoken, the vote went against the Cabinet decision I would resign. It had been thought that a decision would be taken that morning, one way or the other, with a House of Commons majority of about seven, the total majority being larger as the Senate were present and would vote. But effectively it was the House of Commons majority that mattered, as it was they who selected the Parliamentary leader. With the House meeting that afternoon, and several members still wanting to speak, we had to adjourn the discussions till the following day.

That night we had a routine Cabinet meeting which finished at 8 p.m. As it was drawing to an end I turned to Jimmy Chichester-Clark and asked him whether he would like a bed at Stormont House. He had a long drive home and I was under the impression that he had something on in his Ministry early the following morning. At first he accepted and then changed his mind as he thought his wife would expect him to come home. The Minister of Education, overhearing the conversation, said he would come instead. The Cabinet meeting soon ended and I returned to Stormont House with an unexpected guest. It later transpired that several ministers stayed behind at Stormont Castle for a talk and a drink. At 10 p.m. I received intelligence that Jimmy had assured his colleagues that he would stick by them through the second day's Party meeting. This was good news.

The following morning, Wednesday, 23 April, I was just driving off from Stormont Castle when I saw Jimmy arriving in his official car. At first I waved, imagining that he was coming to see someone in the Cabinet offices, but then I could see by the look on his face that he was a worried man. I jumped out and he explained that he must see me at once in my room. Pointing out that we had little time before the meeting started, we conversed standing up. 'I just can't go through with it,' he said. I reminded him that he had sat through yesterday's Party meeting and that the night before he had seemed relaxed and calm. 'Well,' he said, 'I just can't go through with it.' I asked whether he would abstain or absent himself from the Party meeting. 'No,' he replied, 'I must vote against it.' He then hastened to add that he would not join Craig or be a critic of other government policy, but that he must oppose 'one man one vote'. The word 'must' had sinister implications and has never adequately been explained, though I have been given reasons why there was a change between 9.30 p.m. on Tuesday, 22 April, and 10.45 a.m. on Wednesday, 23 April.

Before the vote was taken that morning I thought it right to announce that the Minister of Agriculture had resigned just before the meeting had started in case MPs should vote under any misapprehension. There was a low whistle of surprise. The mere fact that Jimmy voted against the Government reduced the expected majority from seven to five. I think it probable that his defection carried one other person with him and this reduced the Parliamentary majority to three. The whole matter was confused by the presence of the Senate, and this made the majority six. But the important fact to remember is that, as at Westminster, the Parliamentary Party elects the Parliamentary leader and the Senate, like the House of Lords, has no hand in the election. Faulkner also voted against 'one man one vote'.

As Chichester-Clark came out of the Party meeting a close friend of mine went up to him and said, 'This is the worst day for Ulster. What you have done may lead to its downfall.' He laughed it off. The Parliamentary reporter of the *Irish Times,* Fergus Pyle, questioned Jimmy about his actions and in the following morning's paper he is quoted as having said to him, 'It might encourage militant Protestants even to bloodshed.' So whatever pressures were applied I now knew the reasons for the resignation.

That afternoon I stood at the Despatch Box for the last time and announced 'one man one vote'. Looking back I am glad that these were the last words I spoke at Stormont. In my remarks I said, 'I ask all honourable members to rise above sectional partisanship today, for our future, our livelihood are all in danger; and if we go over the brink to disaster all we will have will be equal rights in poverty and despair.'

The following day, Thursday, we had a late night sitting. I decided to have a chat with Billy Fitzsimmons, one of the ministers whom I trusted most, and who was not involved in the legislation which kept us up late. I knew he would fight against any possibility of my giving up the premiership. And so it proved. He was in my room at Parliament Buildings for about one hour. I still remember a remark he made. 'You are', he said, 'trusted by the Catholics, and without you we shall go down to disaster.' However, under pressure he reluctantly admitted that if one of my supporters changed sides my Parliamentary majority would drop to one—an impossible situation. In the end he reluctantly allowed that I must have the right to decide in a case of this kind. What had started as a friendly chat ended by my being more and more insistent as he resisted my suggestions; I suppose this is human nature! In any case, my mind was made up.

The following day I invited Bertie Porter and the Attorney General down to lunch at Stormont House. I quite forgot that a British Legion sale was in progress in the House and we had to eat beside the kitchen. Porter was just as strongly 'against', but the Attorney was more comprehending. They had both been involved the night before in the late sitting, so none of us were at our best. But by the end of the meal they had both agreed that I should be free to go if I wanted to.

A difficult week ending in a late night is not the best formula for feeling fighting fit. That evening I drove home for the weekend. After dinner there was a mighty explosion and the whole house shook. It sounded as if it had come from Lough Neagh about five miles (as the crow flies) from our home. I dashed out and asked the policeman if he had seen anything. 'Yes,' he replied, 'a ball of fire passed over the house.' This, I felt, must be a portent of some kind! It was, in fact, a meteorite which had come up from the direction of Wales on its way North. Dropping pieces as it went, it finally fell into the Atlantic north of County Antrim.

On Saturday a certain amount of telephoning took place. Some people urged me to stay and one person urged me to go quickly if I was going!

On Sunday afternoon I met various friends in the Cabinet at Stormont House. They felt on balance that the man they would best like to serve under would be Jack Andrews. Since Faulkner's resignation he had become No 2 in the Cabinet. He was the leader of the Senate and the son of a former Prime Minister. Perhaps the thought of having to move back from the Senate to the Commons, from which he had retired a few years previously, deterred him, but for whatever reason he declined to allow his name to go forward. I told my friends that I could play no further part in all this, that they would have to decide what to do next, but that the more they delayed the less effect they would have on the ultimate decision.

At about 10 o'clock that night they rang to say that most of the Cabinet were now decided on Chichester-Clark and they hoped I would agree with this decision, even though he had 'stabbed me in the back'. This was a quotation from what my daughter Anne had said when interviewed by reporters on her return from New Zealand to Australia. Shown by a reporter the news that Chichester-Clark had resigned, she was quoted over here as having said, 'Poor Daddy has been stabbed in the back!'

The following morning Chichester-Clark came to see me and I told him the position. He was, I think, genuinely upset that he had set all this in motion and in fact the worried look which I had seen on his face five days earlier when he had resigned as Minister of Agriculture was not to leave it until he resigned as Prime Minister twenty-two months later. I don't think, though, that he had any idea what he was in for.

That afternoon I gave a large tea-party in the Cabinet Room for all those in Parliament who had supported me most ardently. I read out to them the press announcement saying that I was resigning the leadership of the Party. I wanted them to hear it from my own lips before they read it in the paper. All this took place under the eagle eye of Disraeli whose portrait had dominated our Cabinet meetings for some years. Not only do I admire his achievements, but I felt that his Jewish origins should remind us during our deliberations that you could be something other than a Catholic or a Protestant!

The furious lobbying that continued for the next few days, while I still remained Prime Minister, left me largely on one side. Fortunately I had various engagements to carry out, planned long before, and I continued to fulfil them. I did not, however, enter the House of Commons again. One morning Jean and I visited Harland & Wolff. This yard, which we had saved from bankruptcy some two years previously, had been physically transformed. Sir John Mallabar, who had done an industrial doctor's job in Ruston & Hornsby, was brought in to try to achieve a similar result in this vast yard. He soon made friends with Sir William Swallow, the new head of the Shipbuilding Industry Board, and between them they created one of the finest yards in the world. A vast crane from Krupps now dominates Belfast as it strides over an enormous building dock where a one-million-ton ship could be built and floated out when finished.

The vast increase in wages in the Upper Clyde some two years after Jack Mallabar took over sounded the death knell of his efforts. But the physical transformation which he wrought is his finest memorial. He and his wife, Pat, used to live in a flat in the middle of the yard. No one had ever done that before.

It was thrilling to go up the crane on a lift and survey the still incomplete building dock. The only thing which spoilt the visit slightly were the hordes of cameramen.

We also visited and opened the new Commission for developing Antrim and Ballymena. This being so close to home was also a very pleasant chore, though being among one's friends and neighbours it was perhaps a particularly sad occasion.

My last job was on the evening of Wednesday, 30 April. Jim Malley and I visited the Newsboys Club near the centre of Belfast. It was a joint Catholic-Protestant institution. One elderly Catholic walked across the floor before the 'show' had started and just as I was about to take my seat. With tears flowing down his cheeks he held on to my hand and then, with worried officials trying to move him, he muttered, 'thank you'. It was as if he was saying thank you from all the Catholics in Belfast. If at that moment the whole thing was a bit embarrassing, it was nevertheless something that has stuck in my memory ever since, while the rest of that evening has faded into the general memory of yet another function like so many others I had attended during the six years which were now drawing to their close.

The following morning, Thursday, 1 May, was the day the Party was meeting to choose its new leader. I was told that Chichester-Clark would have a majority of five over Faulkner and someone queried whether I ought to attend and vote as the outgoing Prime Minister. From all I had heard, Sir Alec Douglas-Home had voted when Mr Heath was chosen and I was convinced that as an MP I had every right to attend and vote. In the event Chichester-Clark got a majority of one: Faulkner must have been working very hard. If I had not attended, there would have been a dead heat! In a sense it seemed odd that I should vote for the man who had brought me down, but it had been due to worries and doubts in his very unpolitical mind. At Westminster he would have been one of the knights of the shires—though not, I think, a member of the Monday Club. But in any event, I couldn't have brought myself to vote for the man who had been trying to bring me down for six years. It was as simple as that.

After lunch I went round to Government House and offered my resignation as Prime Minister. Although the Governor seemed anxious about the future, and I had to stay much longer than I expected, I do not intend to reveal what occurred in view of certain subsequent events. I went back to Stormont Castle where a large farewell party was already in progress in the upstairs Conference Room, well away from the Cabinet-making, now in full progress in and around my old sitting room. But even this farewell party was not to proceed un-interrupted. Having arrived late I was soon hauled downstairs to speak to a particularly loyal colleague who refused to serve in the new administration unless it had my approval. I told him where I thought his duty lay and by the time I returned the guests were few and far between.

So on 1 May 1969 I laid down what had increasingly become totally impossible burdens. I had won the trust of the Catholics as no previous Prime Minister had ever been able to do, but I was unable to restore to them the rights which small-minded men had removed from them during the first few years of Northern Ireland's existence. Although I was descended from Sir Arthur Chichester, the founder of Belfast, as was my successor, I was also descended from the O'Neills through the female line. Because of my name and my attitude to the minority they could accept me and identify with my aspirations. In a country where you can tell whether a person is a 'Gael' or a 'planter' by his name, this was important. But the party would not allow me to use the advantages I had so as to ensure that Northern Ireland would continue as a respected part of the UK. The Catholics who joined the Unionist Party in my day left it sometime after the August 1969 riots. Because I think it relevant I now print in full the farewell broadcast which I made on Tuesday, 29 April, two days before I left Stormont Castle:

I am speaking to you tonight as your Prime Minister for the last time. As you know, I have resigned the leadership of the Unionist Party and, as soon as my successor is elected, I will be giving up the premiership.

To those of you who have so loyally supported me, who in times of trouble have sent me countless letters, telegrams and other messages, I want to say this: Do not be dismayed. What you and I were trying to do together was right. Morally right, politically right, right for our country and all who seek to live in peace within it.

Justice, equality, generosity—these are enduring standards, and it is far more important to proclaim them than to sit on the fence, wondering which way to jump. But any leader who wants to follow a course of change can only go so far. For change is an uncomfortable thing to many people, and inevitably one builds up a barrier of resentment and resistance which can make further progress impossible.

In my judgment—and in that of my good friends whom I have consulted—I have reached that moment. What is now impossible for me may be—I do not know—easier for someone else. But I have no regrets for six years in which I have tried to break the chains of ancient hatreds. I have been unable to realise during my period of office all that I had sought to achieve. Whether, now, it can be achieved in my life time I do not know. But one day these things will be and must be achieved.

All arguments about the form and personnel of Government are irrelevant when matched against one simple truth. Here we are, in this small country of ours, Protestant and Catholic committed by history to live side by side. No solution based on the ascendancy of any section of our community can hope to endure. Either we live in peace, or we have no life worth living.

For too long we have been torn and divided. Ours is called a Christian country. We could have enriched our politics with our Christianity; but far too often we have debased our Christianity with our politics. We seem to have forgotten that love of neighbour stands beside love of God as a fundamental principle of our religion. I was moved, as many of you must have been, to see the leading clergy of Derry, Protestant and Roman Catholic, side by side in the streets of that troubled city. This simple act of Christian friendship was a shining example of what would have been possible, but for the machinations of wicked men who have preached and practised hatred in the name of God.

A few short weeks ago you, the people of Ulster, went to the polls. I called that Election to afford you the chance to break out of the mould of sectarian politics once and for all. In many places, old fears, old prejudices and old loyalties were too strong.

Yet I am not amongst those who say that the Election served no useful purpose. For it did allow me, with my loyal colleagues, to proclaim a new Declaration of Principles which now binds every Unionist returned to Parliament. It speaks in clear terms of justice and equality; it commits the Party, in honour and in conscience, not merely to do nothing to enlarge the divisions of our community, but to work positively to end them. You will be watching, as I will be, to see to it that these pledges are honoured.

There *is* no other course. Democratic government must rest upon the consent not just of those who elect the governing party, but of the people as a whole. And I remind you once again, as I have done so often before, that Ulster is not a rich, powerful independent state, but a part of the United Kingdom committed to United Kingdom standards and subject in the last resort to United Kingdom authority. We *must* go forward; for British public and parliamentary opinion would not tolerate our going back.

And now the time has come for me to say farewell. My wish for you—for the Province we all love so much—is for peace. We must pray for peace and we must also work for it: the politician in Parliament, the clergy in the churches, the working people in our farms and factories. Look about you at the present state of our country, and try to answer the question: 'Is this *really* the kind of Ulster that you want?' I asked you that question once before; and now, as then, it is only you who can answer.

There is a tendency for everyone to regard politics in personal terms. Even today people who talk to me show by their remarks that they imagine that I would still love to be back in office again. They find it hard to understand that if I am sad about the situation in Northern Ireland it is not because I am no longer Prime Minister of Northern Ireland, but because such utter folly, on so many sides, has led to the situation in which we find ourselves today. Though it may be hard for people to comprehend, 'yesterday's men' do actually think about more important things than loss of office.

13

 After Resignation

SUNDAY, 4 May: I flew to London on my way to Toronto. When I arrived at Belfast Airport I was astonished to see hordes of photographers. I was still apparently not yet a private citizen. 'What,' I was asked, 'did I think of the new Cabinet?' I replied that, as I had hoped, the 'O'Neill' Cabinet was still in existence. In fact, Chichester-Clark had brought two extremists into the Government though not into the Cabinet. One of these, John Taylor, was a liberal at heart, but like Bill Craig, chose to adopt an extremist position, and in consequence had severed his close friendship with Austin Currie, a prominent member of the Nationalist Party. He was to find his way into the Cabinet before long, and since Faulkner became Prime Minister has been followed by his stable mate, John Brooke. It is now no longer possible to say that the Cabinet complexion has not changed. It is more acceptable to extreme Unionist opinion. The Party organisation has also swung to the right and but for London pressure one can well imagine what would happen.

Arrived in London I was met by Tommy Roberts who had done so much for Ulster in Fleet Street. He took me to his home for lunch and then back again to catch the plane to Toronto. While hunting for my tourist seat I saw a photographer searching for me in the first class compartment, and eventually he found me. 'Daily Mail, sir,' he said, 'I thought you would be bound to be first class!' In Toronto once again there was VIP treatment, obviously I was going to be let down gently. Everyone everywhere was kindness itself. There was, however, a surprise in store. I was driven to a hotel in Toronto and booked in under an assumed name. 'Front Page Challenge' was a popular TV guessing game, and no one must know I was in Toronto. A lady from CBC called and said that I could be taken for a drive the next day, but must not be seen on the streets. However, in the end I talked her into allowing me to contact the Eaton family—

distinguished Canadians of Ulster descent—and I was allowed to go and have lunch with one of the younger members of the family at the Toronto Club. This, coupled with a visit to the British Trade Commission, helped to pass the day. That night at dinner, before the show, I was delighted to meet Bob Stanfield, the leader of the Conservative Party. If ever one of nature's gentlemen strayed into politics, the name of that man is Stanfield.

After dinner I was told I would be on the programme first and that Stanfield would follow. This popular programme forced a panel to guess who one was. One stepped out on to a platform and if the audience recognised one they clapped. Then the panel who could not see you, had to guess who you were by asking questions. I felt sure the Canadian audience would not recognise me—after all, Northern Ireland is a tiny speck on the vast surface of the British Commonwealth. In fact, however, there was deafening applause as I emerged. To try and delay the panel's speed of guessing I put on a slight transatlantic accent, but to no purpose. About the third question was, 'Are you from England?' My helpful reply was, 'Not quite.' Then there was a mad rush—'Oh, I know,' 'Oh God, oh, what's his name, oh, oh, O'Neill!' I enjoyed the fifteen minutes questioning. It had been my intention to watch Stanfield through his ordeal, but as I came out of the studio I was told that several other Toronto stations wanted me to go to them at once. I was then raced round about six studios till 11 p.m. When I got back to my hotel there was yet another TV crew outside my bedroom door. It was hard to appreciate that I had resigned.

From Toronto I went to New York where I went on the TV 'Today Show' (upon which our sound model is based), to be interviewed by Hugh Downes and Barbara Walters. I always find American TV much more relaxed than ours, and as usual I enjoyed the show, the informal atmosphere, and the interview. It is only sad to think that my gloomy warnings were to eventuate even more quickly than I had imagined.

I had lunch with the *New York Times* which wrote a good leader on Northern Ireland in which they expressed the hope that my successor would have better luck than I had. Little did they realise how his luck would shape out in August 1969! From there I went on to lunch with the State Department in Washington which cannot now claim that it did not know what to expect! Though, once again, my predictions were the palest reflection of what actually happened four months later.

It was lovely to be in America again. Other people may have some anti-American sentiments; I find it hard to harbour them. On my frequent visits to America I got to know and like Americans and often wonder if the proverbial man-in-the-street in Britain realises how much we owe to them. I had a feeling that this might be my last visit to America. Little did I realise that my wife and I would find ourselves there later that year on a University lecture tour, and that I would be there twice the following year on business trips. I hope that somehow or other I shall continue to visit America for a long time to come.

Soon after my return we went to spend a weekend with the Douglas-Homes in Scotland. He, like everyone else, was glad to know that everything seemed peaceful in Ulster. 'I imagine,' he said, 'that everything will be exactly the same as it was before.'

At home the papers were full of letters expressing joy that peace had returned to the Province—'We always knew there would be peace once O'Neill had gone.' Not one of them realised that my final announcement from the Despatch Box about the introduction of 'one man one vote' in local authority elections had removed the chief *raison d'être* of the Civil Rights movement. Moreover, responsible leaders of the movement, like John Hume, were getting worried by the increasing extremist infiltration of their organisation. But the peace was to be short lived.

Others have written about the details of the August riots and so I would not propose to discuss them other than from a long term point of view. It was these riots which involved the British Army for the first time, and from that time Northern Ireland has, in fact, always been under at least semi-direct rule from London. Previously security had been a matter for the Stormont Government; now, with a Cyprus situation on its hands, the Ministry of Defence was the Ministry responsible for security in this part of the UK. Far the most serious results from this civil war situation was the hatred it engendered. Starting in Derry after the celebrations on 12 August, it soon spread to other centres, notably Belfast. Here some five hundred houses were burnt down and ten people were killed in the streets. With the British Army coming in, almost too late, further arson and bloodshed were avoided—at least for the time being.

Both sides were stunned. Nothing like this had happened for at least a generation. It produced for the Northern Ireland Government a trip to Downing Street, followed by the 'Downing Street Declaration'. But to my mind far the most significant post-riot events were the Home Secretary's visits to Ulster after the Downing Street visit. Jim Callaghan arrived with the head of the London police, Sir Arthur Young, and a programme of reforms in his briefcase. He strode about the place in a commanding attitude, and carried all before him. I have no doubt that, had he wanted to, he could have imposed direct rule there and then. Time alone will show whether this was one of the missed opportunities of Irish history. Certainly what has happened since could not have been worse. Nevertheless, whether due to his Celtic ancestry or not, he was better able to understand how to deal with the 'planters' and 'Gaels' of Ulster than many other British politicians. What I think everybody failed to understand is that you cannot have a situation where Catholic houses are burnt down and Catholics are shot in the street and then say, 'Here are some reforms, let's forget about the past.' Though the reforms were needed they haven't, at least up to the present, been accepted. The minority know that they were ordered from London and the majority, in a condescending manner, call them 'concessions'.

14

Reflections

A FTER the war there was in London great gratitude to Northern
Ireland for the part she had played in the war. Attlee and
Morrison had both been members of Churchill's War Cabinet
and Morrison was now Home Secretary, the head of the Department
which dealt with Ulster's affairs. When in 1949 Eire abruptly left the
Commonwealth, following wartime neutrality, London felt obliged to
introduce legislation to tidy up the after effects of her hurried exit.
At that time Southern Irish emigration to Britain was running at a
very high level. If nothing had been done all these emigrants would
have been aliens. In addition, obviously something would have to be
done to still the understandable fears that now existed in Northern
Ireland about its constitutional future. Under the Government of Ireland Act 1920 there was to have been a Parliament of Southern Ireland
and a Parliament of Northern Ireland with a Council of Ireland as a bridging device between the two. Seventy-five per cent of
that Act never functioned. Only the Parliament of Northern Ireland
came into operation. True, a different Parliament of Southern Ireland
emerged later after 'the Treaty' had been signed, but this was only
after much misery and bloodshed. The South had by then passed
through three stages. First, she had had 'dominion status' and been
known as the 'Irish Free State'. Second, after the abdication of Edward
VIII, De Valera had just kept her in the Commonwealth by renaming
her 'Eire' and keeping a link with Britain under the 'External Relations Act'. Then, when she had become a foreign country, various
ideas were considered to deal with the problems which arose for
Northern Ireland.

In the end she was given a guarantee in the Ireland Act 1949 that
she should remain an integral part of the UK, so long as the Parliament of Northern Ireland so desired. The Unionist Party was quite
misled by this unexpected reinforcement of Northern Ireland's con-

stitutional position. The fact that it was granted by a Labour Government made them feel that they had nothing further to worry about.

It was quite obvious that this 'great gratitude' to Northern Ireland on the part of the British people would slowly fade from their memories. It was also obvious, as I have already pointed out, that Northern Ireland's post-war Education Act, based on the Butler Act, would produce a new Catholic intelligentsia which would be quite unwilling to put up with the deprived status their fathers and grandfathers had taken for granted. But most of the Unionist Party, not least my predecessor, thought the good old days would just rumble on for ever. A heavy price was to be paid for this attitude. It was not until the start of the Civil Rights movement—a picnic compared to what happened in August 1969 and beyond—that the more intelligent members of the Party realised that this problem had to be dealt with. By then it was too late.

As the Party would never stand for change, I was really reduced to trying to improve relations between North and South; and in the North itself between the two sections of the community. In this regard I think I can truthfully say that I succeeded. During this period between 1965 and 1968 the Catholics came to realise that I was interested in their welfare. While the South began to take an interest in the North. The *Irish Times* sent a correspondent, Fergus Pyle; as he had been educated in the North, he understood us better than many Southerners. Today the *Irish Times* gives a better Parliamentary report of what takes place at Stormont than any Northern paper.

There are a lot of Southern Irish in London and I constantly meet them in the street. I often ask them what they used to think of the North in the days when it was possible for these good relations to exist. They always reply that they looked on the North with envy and hoped that in some mysterious way the South could get the advantages of closer association with Britain in the future. But they confess that they no longer hold those views today. August 1969 has changed all that. Today that envy of the North has vanished. It is one of the casualties of the Northern riots and also of the worsening feeling between Catholics and Protestants.

A catalogue of events; someone's life story; these may or may not be of interest. But what, you may well ask, was the thread running through my thoughts and actions during my six years at the helm in Northern Ireland? Many people at home, on both sides of the religious divide, supported me without fully understanding what I was trying to achieve. Today the fact that such aspirations, based on a policy of peace, have proved impossible of attainment, is no reason why I should not outline them for the interested reader.

Had it been possible to make progress towards my goal, then both North and South would have benefited without bloodshed; while Great Britain would have been delighted to have presided over a happier Anglo-Irish relationship. Those of us who have had the opportunity to visit Canada soon discover that, like Australia, she is governed on a federal basis. Most British people are quite ignorant of this fact because they have never known any parliament except the one at Westminster.

I soon became an advocate of regional parliaments, at least for Scotland and Wales, and perhaps later for the various English regions. It seemed to me that if Scotland and Wales, with their Celtic origins, had parliaments of their own they would soon start meeting and talking with the Parliament in Dublin. Northern Ireland would also become involved and eventually a kind of regional parliamentary federation would grow up. It never occurred to me for a moment that the Irish Republic could or would ever come back into the United Kingdom, but I did think she might be able to play an increasingly important role within the British Isles.

All of this, of course, was based on the hope that the lid would not blow off the pot and make further co-operation, in Northern Ireland, impossible. As soon as the Civil Rights movement got under way further progress based on peace became impossible. From then on the pattern which developed was one of rioting, followed by British intervention, followed by forced reforms. A sad way to make progress, and a sure way of making the provincial government at Stormont lose standing with both sides. Eventually somehow, somewhere, peace will break out. Whether this will be a lasting peace or whether there will be a period of peace followed by more bloodshed will depend on the wisdom of the Government in London. Britain's record of dealing with Ireland right from Queen Victoria down to the present day has not been very successful.

Would Gladstone's Irish policies have succeeded had he been allowed to carry them out? The only tangible result of his courage was to sow the seeds for the break up of the Liberal Party. While the problems are almost unmanageable, the British people, and especially the English people, start with a serious disadvantage. They do not understand how the Irish mind, North or South, Protestant or Catholic, works. The English minister imagines that he is dealing with people who think like him. A whole vast Irish vocabulary of expressions is incomprehensible. To him the 'Tricolour' is not the Irish Republican flag, but the French flag. 'No surrender' and 'Not an inch' are not expressions he has heard before. Only if my mythical Englishman has been brought up in Liverpool will he have some slight understanding of the problems with which he is dealing.

Finally, there is one trait in the Irish character which the British find hardest of all to understand. When the Irish are with you they want to please you. By Irish standards it is not misleading to tell someone what he wants to hear. In addition he has a sense of humour and wants to get on with his host or his guest almost at any price. It is in some or all of these ways that the English find the Irish difficult to deal with.

So far as Northern Ireland is concerned, she could have continued to enjoy her privileged position of being the only part of Ireland to enjoy a British standard of living. Instead she chose to put all this at risk in the interests of maintaining a Protestant ascendancy that had ceased to have any meaning anywhere else in the United Kingdom.

Postscript

I N the preface to this book I said that I had virtually completed it
before the introduction of Direct Rule and while I do not want to
alter anything which I have already written I think I would like
to add some general remarks now that the Regional Parliament of
Northern Ireland has been suspended.

I have already explained that as the Unionist Party were unwilling to
contemplate change I was largely, though not entirely, reduced to improving relations between Catholics and Protestants in Northern Ireland and also relations between Northern Ireland and Southern Ireland.
Why then did neither of my successors succeed when reform was
forced upon them by Westminster? Because in my view neither of
them was able to win the trust and confidence of the Catholics. Nor
was this only due to the fact that their names were of British rather than
Irish origin. We all know that in Government circles precedent is a
very important matter. They could have benefited from the ice breaking precedent, which I had created, by visiting Catholic schools and
Catholic hospitals, but they were too frightened of offending their
Protestant followers. I am not conscious that I ever saw a photograph
of either of them in the company of a priest or a nun.

To all this the English reader may well reply—'So what.' About a
year after my resignation I pointed this out to an influential person in
Northern Ireland and this indeed was his actual reply. But in fact
anyone who really understands the Irish character will know that
these matters are of the utmost importance. Not only were the people
in these schools and hospitals delighted to see me, but they also noted
that I came among them, as I went everywhere in Northern Ireland,
without a detective, or indeed protection of any kind.

Some eighteen months after my resignation I met an SDLP MP at a
function in Belfast. 'Well,' I said, 'you are getting your reforms now:
reforms which I was unable to give you.' His reply astonished me. He

said, 'Yes, but we are not accepting them.' When I pressed him further he added 'this lot do not want us to have them'. I think this shows that an attitude of mind is almost as important as the introduction of a reform. The opposition MPs knew perfectly well that both Chichester-Clark and Faulkner had voted aaginst the introduction of one man one vote in local Government elections at the crucial Party meeting where I managed by three votes to win its acceptance. This they felt was what the Unionist Party stood for and wanted, and even if they did not believe the rumours they read in their papers. They knew from past attitudes that the reforms must have been forced on the Government by Jim Callaghan, the Labour Home Secretary.

In fact after August 1969 the sale of reforms to the Unionist Party was a comparatively easy matter. Callaghan had made it perfectly plain to the Ulster Government, in an avuncular manner, that they had two choices. Either they would accept guidance and direction from him or else they would be abolished. In a small place like Northern Ireland, to be a Minister, a Privy Councillor, and to drive about in a Government car is status, and in addition, for many of them the salary is indispensable. The choice presented to the Unionist MPs was: did they want to stay on as MPs drawing their salaries and enjoying their status, or did they want to face the possibility of the closure of Parliament? This was a powerful force acting in favour of reform.

So while not wanting to be too critical, particularly of Chichester-Clark, I do think that with the threat of a London suspension hanging over their heads to ease the passage of reform, it might have been possible for the bridges which I had built between the two sections of the community to be repaired and maintained.

It is always dangerous to look into a crystal ball, but I will certainly be surprised if Stormont is ever re-created, at least in its present form. The imposition of Direct Rule should in my opinion have come in August or September 1969. But as I said in a letter to *The Times* in March 1972 on the morning of Faulkner's fatal visit to Downing Street: 'The calendar has been scattered with dates when action could have been taken.' So if the government are now finding the going hard they have no one to blame but themselves. They dillied and dallied for so long that when they finally intervened the situation was nearly impossible.

But so far as the man they selected to do the job is concerned I have nothing but praise. If there is one person who might 'bring it off', that person is Willie Whitelaw. He has so far received remarkably little help from the former Northern Ireland Government ministers. At the moment of writing Faulkner has just sat on a platform beside Bill Craig and just been to a Press Gallery lunch at Westminster to denigrate Mr Whitelaw. In a strange way I feel he has let me down, for I was asked in London early in 1972 how I thought Faulkner would behave if Direct Rule were introduced, and my reply was that I thought he was a realist and would go along with the British Government especially as, in English terms, he is a dedicated Conservative. I was wrong. Of course this does not mean that by the time these words appear he will not have completely changed course. Of one thing, however, I am certain: Faulkner will go down in history as the man who introduced internment. Indeed historians will note the almost personal terms in which the announcement was made. Gone was the old Chichester-Clark formula which went something like this: 'We will not shrink from introducing internment if this is the advice of the Security Forces.' In political terms, and Brian is nothing if not a political animal, it extended the duration of his premiership from six months to one year. He became a Protestant hero overnight when the announcement was made, and it was not till the end of 1971 that some discerning Protestants began to wonder whether it was turning out all right. In fact it made a very difficult problem virtually insoluble.

The real problem was that Brian had boasted for so long that he was the man who had dealt with the IRA in the late '50s that he had come to believe his own propaganda. When Chichester-Clark resigned the Cabinet at Westminster heaved a sigh of relief. They felt that the political agility of his successor would keep them out of getting too deeply involved in these inexplicable Irish matters. Furthermore, Faulkner, who is the best public relations man I have ever met, sold himself to the Home Office and to Downing Street in a way that his predecessor could not have started to contemplate. In addition the Press fell for him lock, stock and barrel. Meanwhile, the ghastly failure of internment was only finally brought home to London on Bloody Sunday in Derry at the start of 1972. From that moment on, faith in Faulkner started to falter in London. I shall be very surprised if history will be as kind to him as were the London establishment figures in the Spring and Summer of 1971.

So now as I finally bring these memoirs to a close I wonder what the future will bring. The recent past has been so terrible that I find it hard to forecast anything remotely reassuring. The sad thing is that there are so many people on both sides of the great religious divide who fail to appreciate that but for the presence of the British Army a civil war would have been raging for the last two or three years. One of these days the hatreds and suspicions in Ireland will have to be brought to an end. Let us hope it will be sooner rather than later.

Appendix I

THE text of the 'Crossroads' broadcast on BBC and ITA networks, 9 December 1968.

Ulster stands at the crossroads. I believe you know me well enough by now to appreciate that I am not a man given to extravagant language. But I must say to you this evening that our conduct over the coming days and weeks will decide our future. And as we face this situation, I would be failing in my duty to you as your Prime Minister if I did not put the issues, calmly and clearly, before you all. These items are far too serious to be determined behind closed doors, or left to noisy minorites. The time has come for the people as a whole to speak in a clear voice.

For more than five years now I have tried to heal some of the deep divisions in our community. I did so because I could not see how an Ulster divided against itself could hope to stand. I made it clear that a Northern Ireland based upon the interests of any one section rather than upon the interests of all could have no long-term future.

Throughout the community many people have responded warmly to my words. But if Ulster is to become the happy and united place it could be there must be the will throughout our Province and particularly in Parliament to translate these words into deeds.

In Londonderry and other places recently, a minority of agitators determined to subvert lawful authority played a part in setting light to highly inflammable material. But the tinder for that fire, in the form of grievances real or imaginary, had been piling up for years.

And so I saw it as our duty to do two things. First, to be firm in the maintenance of law and order, and in resisting those elements which seek to profit from any disturbances. Secondly, to ally firmness with fairness, and to look at any underlying causes of dissension which were troubling decent and moderate people. As I saw it, if we were not prepared to face up to our problems, we would have to meet mounting pressure both *internally*, from those who were seeking change, and *externally* from British public and parliamentary opinion, which had been deeply disturbed by the events in Londonderry.

That is why it has been my view from the beginning that we should decide—of our own free will and as a responsible Government in command of events—to press on with a continuing programme of change to secure a united and harmonious community. This, indeed, has been my aim for over five years.

Moreover, I knew full well that Britain's financial and other support for Ulster, so laboriously built up, could no longer be guaranteed if we failed to press on with such a programme.

I am aware, of course, that some foolish people have been saying: 'Why should we bow the knee to a Labour Prime Minister? Let's hold out until a Conservative Government returns to power, and then we need do nothing.' My friends, that is a delusion. This letter is from Mr Edward Heath, and it tells me—with the full authority of the Shadow Cabinet and the expressed support of my old friend Sir Alec Douglas-Home—that a reversal of the policies which I have tried to pursue would be every bit as unacceptable to the Conservative Party. If we adopt an attitude of stubborn defiance we will not have a friend left at Westminster.

I make no apology for the financial and economic support we have received from Britain. As a part of the United Kingdom, we have always considered this to be our right. But we cannot be a part of the United Kingdom merely when it suits us. And those who talk so glibly about acts of impoverished defiance do not know or care what is at stake. Your job, if you are a worker at Short's or Harland & Wolff; your subsidies if you are a farmer; your pension, if you are retired—all these aspects of our life, and many others, depend on support from Britain. Is a freedom to pursue the un-Christian path of communal strife and sectarian bitterness really more important to you than all the benefits of the British Welfare State?

But this is not all. Let me read to you some words from the Government of Ireland Act, 1920—the Act of the British Parliament on which Ulster's Constitution is founded.

'Notwithstanding the establishment of the Parliament of Northern Ireland ... the supreme authority of the Parliament of the United Kingdom shall remain unaffected and undiminished over all persons, matters and things in [Northern] Ireland and every part thereof.'

Because Westminster has trusted us over the years to use the powers of Stormont for the good of all the people of Ulster, a sound custom has grown up that Westminster does not use its supreme authority in fields where we are normally responsible. But Mr Wilson made it absolutely clear to us that if we did not face up to our problems the Westminster Parliament might well decide to act over our heads. Where would our Constitution be then? What shred of self-respect would be left to us? If we allowed others to solve our problems because we had not the guts—let me use a plain word—the guts to face up to them, we would be utterly shamed.

There are, I know, today some so-called loyalists who talk of independence from Britain—who seem to want a kind of Protestant Sinn Fein. These people will not listen when they are told that Ulster's income is £200 million a year but that we can spend £300 million—only because Britain pays the balance.

Rhodesia, in defying Britain from thousands of miles away, at least has an Air Force and an Army of her own. Where are the Ulster armoured divisions or the Ulster jet planes? They do not exist and we could not afford to buy them. These people are not merely extremists. They are lunatics who would set a course along a road which could only lead at the end into an all-Ireland Republic. They are not loyalists but *dis*loyalists: disloyal to Britain, disloyal to the Constitution, disloyal to the Crown, disloyal—if they are in public life—to the solemn oaths they have sworn to Her Majesty The Queen.

But these considerations, important though they are, are not my main concern. What I seek—and I ask for the help and understanding of you all—is a swift end to the growing civil disorder throughout Ulster. For as matters stand today, we are on the brink of chaos, where neighbour could be set against neighbour. It is simple-minded to imagine that problems such as these can be solved by repression. I for one am not willing to expose our police force to indefinite insult and injury. Nor am I prepared to see the shopkeepers and traders of Ulster wrecked and looted for the benefit of the rabble. W must tackle root causes if this agitation is to be contained. We must be able to say to the moderate on both sides: come with us into a new era of co-operation, and leave the extremists to the law. But this I also say to all, Protestant or Roman Catholic, Unionist or Nationalist: disorder must now cease. We are taking the necessary measures to strengthen our police forces. Determined as we are to act with absolute fairness, we will also be resolute in restoring respect for the laws of the land.

Some people have suggested that I should call a General Election.

It would, in my view, be utterly reprehensible to hold an Election against a background of bitterness and strife. I have spoken to you in the past about the groundswell of moderate opinion. Its presence was seen three years ago when we fought an election on a Manifesto which would stand inspection in any Western democracy and we swept the country on a non-sectarian platform. Those who would sow the wind by having a bitter Election now would surely reap the whirlwind.

And now I want to say a word directly to those who have been demonstrating for Civil Rights. The changes which we have announced are genuine and far-reaching changes and the Government as a whole is totally committed to them. I would not continue to preside over an Administration which would water them down or make them meaningless. You will see when the members of the Londonderry Commission are appointed that we intend to live up to our words that this will be a body to command confidence and respect. You will see that in housing allocations we mean business. You will see that legislation to appoint an Ombudsman wil be swiftly introduced. Perhaps you are not entirely satisfied; but this is a democracy, and I ask you now with all sincerity to call your people off the streets and allow an atmosphere favourable to change to develop. You are Ulstermen yourselves. You know we are all of us stubborn people, who will not be pushed too far. I believe that most of you want change, not revolution. Your voice has been heard, and clearly heard. Your duty now is to play your part in taking the heat out of the situation before blood is shed.

But I have a word too for all those others who see in change a threat to our position in the United Kingdom. I say to them, Unionism armed with justice will be a stronger cause than Unionism armed merely with strength. The bully-boy tactics we saw in Armagh are no answer to these grave problems: but they incur for us the contempt of Britain and the world, and such contempt is the greatest threat to Ulster. Let the Government govern and the police take care of law and order.

What in any case are these changes which we have decided must come? They all amount to this: that in every aspect of our life, justice must not only be done but be *seen* to be done to all sections of the community. There must be evident fairness as between one man and another.

The adoption of such reforms will not, I believe, lose a single seat at Stormont for those who support the Unionist cause and indeed some may be gained. And remember that it is with Stormont that the power of decision rests for maintaining our Constitution.

148

And now a further word to you all. What kind of Ulster do you want? A happy and respected Province, in good standing with the rest of the United Kingdom? Or a place continually torn apart by riots and demonstrations, and regarded by the rest of Britain as a political outcast? As always in a democracy, the choice is yours. I will accept whatever your verdict may be. If it is your decision that we should live up to the words 'Ulster is British' which is part of our creed, then my services will be at your disposal to do what I can. But if you should want a separate, inward-looking, selfish and divided Ulster then you must seek for others to lead you along that road, for I cannot and will not do it. Please weigh well all that is at stake, and make your voice heard in whatever way you think best, so that we may know the views *not* of the few *but* of the many. For this is truly a time of decision, and in your silence *all* that we have built up could be lost. I pray that you will reflect carefully and decide wisely. And I ask all our Christian people, whatever their denomination, to attend their places of worship on Sunday next to pray for the peace and harmony of our country.

Appendix II

THE exchange of letters between the Prime Minister and Mr
Brian Faulkner at the time of Mr Faulkner's resignation in
January 1969.

Brian Faulkner's letter of resignation 23 January 1969

You are aware that I have been unhappy about the setting up of the
Commission. It is, in my opinion, a political manoeuvre and to some
extent an abdication of authority, and it is misleading to the Parliamentary Party. The Government is better qualified to decide for itself
what is to be done.

The essential now is strong Government capable of either: 1, gaining
the confidence of the Unionist Party for a change of policy and introducing on its own initiative adult suffrage in the local government
franchise—which I personally believe to be the right course; or 2,
resisting the pressures being brought to bear on the Government.

In either case law and order must be enforced.

This administration falls down on both the alternatives I have
mentioned.

I have remained throughout successive crises when resignation might
have further disrupted the Party. And for the same reasons I have
hesitated now. On reflection, however, I am forced to the conclusion
that not only is the Party tearing itself to pieces, but conditions in the
country are such that the work of my department is imperilled.

In these circumstances I feel I can no longer usefully serve in your
Government and I ask you to accept my resignation.

My reply was as follows:

Thank you for your letter of 23 January, offering your resignation
which I shall tender to His Excellency the Governor.

As you say I was aware of your views on the Commission. I find it, however, rather surprising, if you felt as strongly as you now say you do, that you did not offer to resign when the Cabinet reached its decision in this matter.

You characterise the Commission, which you will note has been commended by the leaders of both major parties at Westminster, as 'a political manoeuvre and to some extent an abdication of authority,' as if it were a step unprecedented in our political system.

In fact it is an action with ample precedent both in Britain and other countries, where there has been serious civil disorder. In a situation in which charge and counter-charge have been exchanged and the truth is obscured I can see great value in an examination by an impartial Commission.

As for abdication of authority, I find it strange that the President of the United States, the most powerful political executive in the world, can set up—as he did—an impartial Commission into civil disorders, while you consider a similar step by our Government to be 'an abdication of authority'.

The main ground on which you base your resignation, however, is the absence of what you term 'strong Government'. I will remind you that it was I, immediately after the events of 5 October in Londonderry, who advised you and all our colleagues that since this was not a situation which could be maintained by 'law and order' means alone changes must be made; and it was you who were one of the principal protagonists of the view that there ought to be no change under what you described as 'duress'. You maintained that attitude up to and beyond our meeting with Mr Wilson; yet after he wrote to us following that meeting you agreed, and were fully committed to, the five points which we announced on 22 November.

It is true that when I recommended the appointment of a Commission you suggested that as an alternative we should go to the Party and tell them that universal adult suffrage must be adopted. But you had earlier expressed the view that the franchise evidently could not be changed in the short term; you specifically approved the statement relating to this issue in the proposals of 22 November and you knew perfectly well, following the Party meeting at which these proposals were discussed, that any change in the declared policy was not acceptable at the present time to the vast majority of our parliamentary colleagues.

And so, the choice with which you presented us when we considered the proposed Commission was either (a) that we should do nothing at all, relying entirely upon 'law and order' methods which had clearly proved inadequate to cope with the situation; or (*b*) that we should go to our Party telling them that we intended to tear up a whole series of policy statements, and knowing full well that they would not support us. Such a suggestion struck me as somewhat disingenuous.

At no time, in all the difficult weeks since 5 October, had you taken any initiative in recommending any measure to take the heat out of the situation. You never came to me, following our decisions of 22 November, to say that in your view the franchise must be changed. I had to wait until I had myself made a positive proposal to lower the temperature—that is, the Commission: and then you produced the two alternatives of doing nothing or of attempting what you must have known to be politically impossible, and therefore, in practice, doing nothing. Hobson's choice!

You also tell me that you remained through what you term 'successive crises'. I am bound to say that if, instead of passively 'remaining' you had on occasions given me that loyalty and support which a Prime Minister has the right to expect from his Deputy, some of these so-called crises might never have arisen.

Only one who has sat in my chair could appreciate how greatly one is sustained in a difficult and lonely office by the support of truly loyal colleagues. If on these earlier occasions to which you refer you took issue with me on some vital points of principle, you should surely have resigned. Alternatively you should have been to the fore in defending the administration. But you did neither: as you yourself so accurately put it you 'remained'.

Finally you speak of 'the party tearing itself to pieces' and the work of your department being imperilled. I ask you to consider this: if you had been willing immediately after 5 October to support me in advocating changes which had to come, instead of talking only in terms of 'strong Government' is it not at least possible that much of this travail could have been prevented?

My object throughout has been to prevent Ulster tearing itself to pieces, and I am convinced that time will show that I have been consistent from start to finish in the policies I have advocated. As you say the essential now and always is strong Government; but this is only possible if Ministers stand together, prepared to be firm where firmness is necessary and fair where fairness is needed.

I am sorry you should be leaving the Ministry of Commerce at a time when the increasingly difficult economic circumstances would fully test your knowledge and experience of that vital department.

In his second letter to me Faulkner wrote:

I have your letter of today's date. Since you have mentioned the question of my attitude at various times in discussion with our colleagues I feel bound to make my position clear.

You say that at the outset you advised our colleagues that changes must be made and you imply that I was one of the number of protagonists of no change. I must remind you that as long ago as 23 October I made it clear that I had no dogmatic views on the franchise. My consistent view has been that we should take firm decisions on issues before us and then accept responsibility ourselves for implementing them.

It was shortly after that you advised our colleagues that they should adhere to the line that the franchise should not be reviewed until after the re-organisation of local government. I find it difficult to understand, therefore, your view that I failed to take the initiative in recommending a specific solution to our difficulties after that time.

More recently you told your colleagues that a change in the franchise was inevitable, that it could well come from the Commission's report. Its implementation therefore was only a matter of time.

My difficulty in these circumstances is that I simply cannot reconcile myself to reiterating pledges that have been given to the Party, namely that there is no change in the Government's policy on this matter.

I am hurt by your reference to lack of support during my period of office. There is much I could say, but I would prefer not to indulge in recrimination.

My final reply to Faulkner:

Thank you for your further letter of 24 January. As you say, recrimination is undesirable, and there would be no question of it if you had not chosen in your resignation letter to describe all your recent colleagues as a weak Government indulging in political manoeuvring and misleading the parliamentary party.

I have no wish to prolong exchanges which can only damage Unionism, but I must be permitted the opportunity of replying to the points raised in your letter of 24 January and to some of the comments which you made in television interviews last night.

You say that on 24 October 1968, you told us that you had no dogmatic views on the franchise. That is so, but nothing is more misleading than partial quotation, and you went on to say—as I reminded you in my letter yesterday—that the franchise evidently could not be changed in the short term. You were not making a firm decision, you were passing an observation.

You go on to recall that I advised our colleagues in public statements, to adopt a consistent line on the franchise issue. But the position was that the Government policy on this issue had been declared, that it evidently could not be changed in the short term, and that one could not have members of the Government, within the context of collective responsibility, publicly disagreeing with each other. You imply that in saying this I deterred you from declaring right away public support for an immediate change. If that was your view it was certainly never communicated to your colleagues.

You also recall that in proposing the appointment of a Commission, I told our colleagues that such a body might well express views on the franchise. I did so because I was anxious to put the proposition to the Cabinet with complete candour, not misleading them in any way about its possible implications. But the Government's policy on the franchise issue remains unaffected; we have promised a review once the pattern for re-organisation of local government is established, and in making that review we shall consider all the revelant factors, including any comments the Commission may make on the subject.

Finally, you say you are hurt by my reference to lack of support from you in the past. Yet on television last night you displayed again that ambiguity which has confused people in the past. Thus you said at different times that you had consistently been behind the Government policies, yet on a number of occasions before had been on the point of resignation. If you were, in fact, consistently behind the Government policies I am at a loss to know what was bringing you so often to the fence of resignation which you failed to jump.

You still seem unable to understand that a Deputy Prime Minister above all can reasonably be expected to show some personal loyalty to the Prime Minister of the day. I do not wish to argue the point. Instead I enclose a transcript of an interview which you gave from America while I was struggling for my political life in 1966. You will see that you were specifically asked to say whether or not you supported me as Prime Minister and that you took refuge in ambiguities about Government policy. Had you been willing to give straight answers to questions such as these on a number of occasions it would both have sustained me and, I am sure, increased respect for you.

Index

O'Neill, Patrick (son), 2, 17, 25, 91, 94, 119
O'Neill, Hon Robert Torrens (great-uncle), 4-5
O'Neill, Shane (brother), 5, 9-10
O'Neill, Sylvia see Rathcavan
O'Neill, Timmy, see Buxton, Timmy

The Observer, 102
'one man one vote' *see* electoral reform
Ormsby-Gore, David (later: Lord Harlech), 48, 51, 52, 56, 57, 60

Paisley, Ian, 63, 78, 84, 98, 105, 109; opposes O'Neill in 1969 elections, 26, 111; and 1970 election victories, 28; protests against Lynch visit, 74; 1966 demonstrations, 80, 87; and goes to jail, 82, 83; Catholic extremists vote for, 120
Parker, Dame Dehra, 32, 33-4
Parsons, Johnny, 87
Pay Roll Tax, 36
Pearson, Lester, 51, 113
Peel, David, 23
People's Democracy (PD), 119, 120; New Year march, 110-11; *see also* Civil Rights
planning *see* economic planning
police protection, 123
Ponsonby, Sir Henry, 3, 4
'Portadown Parliament', 118
Porter, Bertie, 108, 114, 117, 124, 126
Powell, Enoch, O'Neill's meeting (1955), 33, 34
Pyle, Fergus, 125, 137

Queen Elizabeth II Bridge, controversy over naming of, 78
Queen's University, PD movement based on, 110; parliamentary representation by, 114

Rathcavan, Lord (Hugh O'Neill), 13, 26, 90
Rathcavan, Sylvia (neé Sandeman: Terence's aunt), 18, 90
Red Hand (of the O'Neills), 6-7, 54, 64, 102
regional parliaments, O'Neill in favour of, xi-xiii, 138
Reilly, Sir Patrick, 81
Rent De-restriction Bill, 33-4
Rhodesia, 83, 86-7
Roberts, Sir Frank and Lady, 89
Roberts, Tommy, 23, 38, 89, 132
Rockefeller, Governor, 99

Rosebery, Lord, 4
Rowallane National Trust Garden, 41
Royal Hibernian Academy, 37
Rusk, Dean, 57

St Patrick's Protestant Benevolent Society, 56
Salinger, Pierre, 58
Sayers, Jack, 47, 75
Scotch-Irish Society of Philadelphia, 48-9
Second World War, 20-5
Selby, Ralph, 22-3
Selassie, Emperor Haile (Ras Tafari), 14-15
Shanes Castle (O'Neill family home), 1-2, 5-6, 9, 10-14, 26, 111
SHAPE, 64
Sharp, Mitchell, 113
Shelley, Mayor (of San Francisco), 93
Shipbuilding Industry Board, 128
Short Brothers (aircraft factory), 54, 66, 77
Siddons, Mrs Sarah, 11-12
Sinclair, Maynard, 31
Somme Battle celebrations, 78, 80, 81
Soskice, Frank, 6, 82
Southampton, Ulster Trade Week in, 94
Soviet Union, 65, 99
Stanfield, Bob, 133
Strange, Robert, 119
Sunday Independent (Dublin), 112
Swallow, Sir William, 128

Taylor, Dennis, 54
Taylor, John, 61, 132
Ten Horn family (Nijmegen, Holland), 25, 63
Thompson, George, 37
Thompson, Jack, 71, 98
Thomson, Lord, 45
The Times, 19-20, 30, 45, 62, 99, 117
'Today Show' (American TV), O'Neill interviews, 93, 101, 133
Topping, Ken, 34
Transport and General Workers' Union (TGWU), 84
Turtle, Rev David, 115
Tyrone county, electoral control in, 121

Ulster Development Bonds, 39
Ulster Unionist Party, 4, 5, 20, 61; 1970 electoral losses, xiii; O'Neill fails to get candidacy at Larne, 25; and elected member for Bannside (1946), 25-6; Annual Council Meeting (1963), 46-7;

Ulster Unionist Party—*cont.*
  Lemass/O'Neill meeting approved, 73;
  1966 back-bench conspiracy, 84-6, 104,
  117; rivalry between Faulkner and
  Craig, 104-5, 117; controversy over
  'Civil Rights' reforms, 106-7; and unreasonable attitudes, 108, 109; opposition to Cameron Report, 114-15; independent pro-O'Neill MPs, 122; back-
  bench seeks downfall of O'Neill (1969),
  122-3; and O'Neill resigns, 126-31; reaction to Ireland Act (1949), 136-7; *see
  also* elections; electoral reform; 'Portadown Parliament'
Ulster Volunteer Force (UVF), 4, 78, 81,
  123; Malvern Street shooting and, 81-2
Ulster Trade Weeks (in Britain), 64, 66,
  84-5, 94, 102
United States, 88, 102; affinities with
  Northern Irish, xii; troops stationed in
  N. Ireland during war, 20; Scotch-
  Irish in, 48-9; missile gap between
  USSR and, 65; O'Neill's visits: 1963:
  51-2; 1964: 56-9 ;1965: 23, 24, 77;
  1967: 93-4; 1968: 99-100, 101; 1969:
  133-4

Vaughan, Bertie, 119
Victoria, Queen, 138; her dislike of Irish,
  3-4

Wakehurst, Lord, 41, 44
Wales, O'Neill visits Cardiff, 56
Waller, Ian, 115
Walters, Barbara, 93, 133
Warnock, Edmond, 34, 42, 52, 73
Waugh, Auberon, 119
West, Harry, 85, 109; dismissed by
  O'Neill, 92-3
West Downs school, Winchester, 17
West Germany, O'Neill's official visit
  (1967), 88, 89-92
Whitaker, Jean *see* O'Neill, Jean (wife of
  Terence)
Whitaker, Ken, Lemass visit to Belfast
  and, 68-9, 71, 72
Whitworth, A. W., 17, 59, 60
Wilson, Harold, 28, 55, 77, 86, 95, 103,
  119; O'Neill meeting in House of Com-
  mons (1964), 61-2; and at Downing
  Street: 1964: 65; 1966: 82-3; 1967: 88;
  1968: 102, 104, 105; against O'Neill re-
  signing, 113; approves Cameron Com-
  mission, 115
Wilson, Professor Tom, economic plan of,
  52, 67
Wolff, Gustav *see* Harland and Wolff
Woodvale Unionist Association meeting,
  hostile crowd outside, 97-8
World Bank, 36, 38, 51, 68

Young, Sir Arthur, 123, 135